the singles game

by Andrew J. DuBrin, Ph.D.

BOOKS FOR BETTER LIVING • CHATSWORTH, CALIFORNIA

To Marcia

Who changed her surname from Miller
to DuBrin in the interim between the
writing and the publication of this book.

CONTENTS

PREFACE

Finding a partner for sex, love, companionship, and fun—or all four—is a problem that confronts millions of people. Even among those fortunate people who are already receiving some love, sex, or companionship, many say to themselves, "Perhaps I could do a little better." Many people remain attached to their present spouses or lovers simply because they fear the prospects of not being able to find a suitable replacement. Perhaps the majority of adults are at any one point in time looking for a new romantic involvement. These unattached people include in their ranks single people not involved in an exclusive relationship, the separated, divorced, widowed, and those legally married, but who have privately agreed to "shop around." *The Singles Game* is written for people seeking new relationships now or who may be doing so in the future.

My book is not a thinly veiled autobiographical sketch of the first hand experiences of a lecherous male psychologist, author, and professor. However, I have made the effort to directly participate in most of the approaches to meeting people discussed in this book. In gathering material for *The Singles Game*, I have spoken to, or corresponded with, hundreds of people, studied the questionnaire responses of several hundred others, and read many books and magazine articles on the topic. At times, I have even traveled under a pseudonym in order to collect information unobtrusively.

The Singles Game is directed more toward heterosexuals than homosexuals. In general, the approximately one hundred and fifty approaches to meeting people are more applicable to the straight than the gay world. However, gay people should be able to decide which ideas and suggestions contained in this book are useful to them. Straight people will also have to judge which methods will work best for them.

The word "game" in my title is used with considerable thought. Finding sex, love, companionship, and fun can be much more than a chance happening, predetermined by fate. Yet this search does not have the formality of a set of scientific procedures. Finding a partner is an art, skill, or game. My book offers some guidelines or rules for increasing the odds of winning such a game.

Exploitation of men or women, chicanery, manipulation, or brainwashing are not implied in talking about the singles game. Nevertheless, finding a partner suitable to your interests does involve competition. The risk of losing this game is rejection and loneliness. The rewards from winning are sex, love, companionship, and fun.

ACKNOWLEDGEMENTS

Ideas in this book came from many people. Over two hundred people, including students of mine, shared with me their ideas on finding people. Many friends, male and female, have wittingly or unwittingly supplied me with useful information about how opposite sexed adults meet. I read every book or article about meeting people that I or my research associate could uncover. In short, I owe general appreciation to many people, including authors, friends, acquaintances, students, and others who have contributed to this book without realizing they were helping.

Specific appreciation is due several people. Donald F. Biggs, my research associate on this project, gathered information and conducted some revealing interviews. K. Lois Smith typed most of the manuscript, Cindy Harrell pinch hitted in the final stages, while Vicki F. Gary and Barbara S. Wagner performed a variety of crucial secretarial chores. Hedy White, my editor at Books For Better Living, believed in my book and provided me with a variety of astute suggestions.

Above all, thank you Marcia Miller DuBrin for your encouragement during the preparation of this book, and for your variety of keen observations and witty comments about single people.

Andrew J. DuBrin
Rochester, New York

Chapter 1

THE SINGLES LAMENT

"Somewhere out there in that great big world there must be at least one person for me," lament thousands of lonely people. Repeatedly they ask themselves and anybody who might be of help, "How do you meet people?" Sex manuals provide all you need to know about making love. Drug stores will sell you the necessary chemicals or equipment to insure that love-making is recreation, not procreation. Clothing stores can help you appear more attractive to other people. Movies, television shows, and novels convince you (if you need convincing) that romance adds zest to your life. Tragically, it is all wasted until you find a partner of the opposite sex.

Finding a lover, companion, or mate is one of the most important activities in life. Yet more books are written about buying a house or finding a job. An abortion center is easier to locate than a reliable place to meet a man. Do not feel alone if finding people is difficult for you. Marlene, Chet, Ingrid, Dan, and Eunice are typical examples of other people who face the same problem.

Marlene, the Disgruntled School Teacher

Marlene, age 28, was lonely, miserable, and unattached in her hometown. She felt that staying in Lancaster, Pennsylvania would doom her to a single life. Marlene moved to New York in hopes of finding a singles' paradise. Within several months she successfully located a teaching job in the Bronx, a roommate, and a small, expensive apartment on the East Side. Marlene gave up her car and any hopes of saving money. One year later, she returned to Lancaster, lonelier and more depressed than when she left town. Marlene explains what went wrong:

"In terms of meeting men, New York was a disaster. In one year I just had a handful of dates with a few creeps. Almost every man I met wanted to go to bed the first night. One guy insisted we have sex on the couch while my roommate was sleeping in the next room. When I said no, he threatened to tear up my clothing. I finally got him out by promising that my roommate would be out of town next weekend and that we could make love then.

"Maybe my routine prevented me from meeting men. In the morning I would ride that repulsive subway to work. I'd meet characters with bad breath who reached their hands in my coat for a free feel. Once we were stuck for twenty minutes; a man about 60 rubbed himself against me for the whole time. There was just nobody to meet at the public school where I taught. Male faculty members were either married or gay.

"There were so many robberies and rapings in my neighborhood that I was afraid to talk to any people who lived in my apartment building. I had no car, so going out to beaches or lake resorts to meet men was difficult. I tried the singles bar routine, but at my age I felt silly in those places. I tried computer dating and that failed. All I met were a few older men even more desperate than myself.

"Another problem was that I found those New York people peculiar. I had never met such pushy, noisy people before. I felt as if I were visiting a foreign country whenever I was with more than a few New Yorkers at a time. It irritated me when

people kept on saying, 'Are you from out-of-town?'
After awhile, I would say, 'Yes, fortunately.' I
kept hoping that I would meet a fellow from
Pennsylvania, Ohio, or anywhere but New York. I
even asked a few people if there were something
like a Pennsylvania Club in New York.

"It was impossible to meet men through friends
because I found it very difficult to make friends in
the city. Girls are even paranoid toward girls in
New York. All I can tell you is that the city was
a real bummer."

Chet, the Uncool Executive

Chet, an automobile company executive, age 53,
became single again after thirty-one years of marriage. In the executive suite, Chet is a careful
planner and usually has his work under control.
When it comes to business, Chet knows the logic
behind every move he makes. Despite his good income, satisfactory appearance, and executive
skills, Chet's social life is almost bankrupt.
Chet's analysis of his woman-hunt is revealing.

"It was no picnic getting back into social life
after thirty-one years of marriage; Marge and I
hashed over things for two years before we finally
separated. The children are all of college age or
beyond, so we didn't have to contend with breaking
up a family. Nevertheless, it was hell actually
moving out of our big home and moving into an
apartment in the city.

"At first I didn't care about dating. For three
months my only social life was playing golf and
going to the movies by myself. My first attempt at
a real date was to ask a former secretary of mine to
lunch. I paced around the apartment twenty minutes before calling her. When we did get together
for lunch two days later, I felt so awkward that I

was embarrassed to call her again.

"I had read how younger girls think older successful men are attractive, so I thought I would try a few young chicks. Maybe that was a mistake. First of all, it wasn't that easy to find a young girl to ask for a date. It would have looked bad for the company image if I visited the secretarial pool to have coffee with the girls. We do have two young girls in our management trainee program, but that could lead to some complications. Suppose one of the girls I dated were later assigned to my department? I didn't want to have to handle that situation.

"I did ask a girl about 22 from our company art department for a date. She acted as if she didn't understand what I was saying. Then she made some crack like, 'I make it a policy never to date men older than my father. It makes him jealous.' At that point I decided to look for girls off company premises.

"Next, I called a few daughters of business acquaintances of mine. I wasn't crazy enough to ask out teenagers, but I did ask out one girl about 20 who was still living with her parents. She was quite cold on the phone and suggested that I go back to my wife and children. The following day I received a phone call from her father, suggesting that perhaps I should talk things over with my family doctor. The call made me indignant, but as I look back on it, I can't say it was undeserved.

"My last attempt to find a date with a young chick was with Vicki, a friend of my oldest daughter. Vicki refused me in a nice way. She didn't even put me down, but suggested I meet her 50 year old aunt who had recently lost her husband.

"Later that month I met a divorced woman in her forties with three teenage children. We went out a few times. I even took her on a weekend vacation out-of-town. I thought this woman was nice, but she wasn't really what I was looking for. I've been married to a woman in her forties, and I'm looking for a woman somewhat younger. I think what I'll do next is look for a divorcée or a single girl about 30.

Ingrid, the Isolated Biochemist

Ingrid, a 36 year old divorcée, lives with her two young children in a small rural town, twenty miles outside of Indianapolis. She is employed as a biochemist in a pharmaceutical firm within the city. Each morning she gets up at six to ready herself for work, and her children for school. Ingrid's children take care of themselves between the time they arrive home from school and she arrives home from work. Routinely, Ingrid goes to bed alone each night at 10:30. During the past twelve months Ingrid has had one date and no sex. She explains:

"First of all, it's very difficult for a woman in my situation to meet a respectable man. There are just no available men in this town. The only single man I know of over 25 and under 65 is Jeff, an old widower down the road. He lives alone with a few hunting dogs. I just wouldn't consider him a possibility for dating.

"When my husband and I split, he took the only friends we have. They were really his friends. One of them invited me to a dinner party three months after our divorce. I felt very self-conscious attending a dinner party alone when all the other people were married couples. It made me realize that the best thing for me was to get started on a new social life of my own. Getting started proved to be much more difficult than I imagined.

16

"You ask me why I stayed in this small rural town instead of moving to the city where I might be able to meet some men. I'm afraid of moving to the city for the children's sake. Josie and Mike are getting to the age where they might be influenced by older children. I've heard so much about the drug problem in city schools. Besides, there are a lot of knifings and muggings in cities these days.

"I have considered going into the city to attend a club or Parents Without Partners meeting. But it's so hard to get a baby sitter. Also it would be over twenty miles each way. I would get back late on a weekday night to get enough sleep before a long day of hard work.

"I am also a little concerned about dating most men. People have told me that a man who dates a divorced woman expects sex right away. My husband and I had such bad sexual relations for so many years, that I'm hesitant to get involved again. It would have to be something gradual. Besides, I'm not really very good at sex and most men would be disappointed with me.

"There is another serious problem I would face if I started to date a man. After a date, I have to return home because of the children. I certainly cannot entertain men in my house with the children sleeping in the next room. My one date wanted to spend the night with me, right in my own bedroom. Imagine what the children would think if they woke up to find a man in the house. That is no way to bring up children. Especially my daughter. If I sleep with men I'm not married to, what can I expect of her?"

Ray, the Married Hunter

Ray, a 33 year old Boston stockbroker, is unhappily married. Ray and his wife endured the pangs of loneliness associated with a bad marriage for many years. Jointly they reached a decision to keep the family intact, live under the same roof, but maintain separate social lives. Ray was enthusiastic about his new-found freedom to cure his loneliness and simultaneously join the sexual revolution.

A stockbroker on the loose in Boston? How can he miss? All that action downtown and in Harvard Square; and think of those thousands of liberated coeds stalking the streets looking for older men. Lucky Ray, he has reached the apex of living. Single again in a city densely populated with lovely girls.

So far, Ray has had many more misses (and not the female kind) than hits. Allow Ray to ramble on about his modest success in hunting for women.

"I'm not sure what my problem is. I know I'm not Irish-Catholic, but that alone could not have made social life so difficult. After four months of really scraping the barrel, I'm seriously thinking of getting back to my wife. Maybe we can work something out. Having a license to hunt while married isn't all it's cracked up to be. Who wants to come home to an icy stare and a cold bed after hanging out in a bar at night?

"Up to the point where my wife and I decided to go our separate ways, I had nothing more than a casual conversation with another woman. During the day, when the stock exchange is open, I'm almost chained to the phone at my desk. I work in a small branch of our firm, and there just don't seem to be as many possibilities in the office for meeting women. My first attempt at making an actual date was to approach Marie, a girl in the research department.

"Her response was, 'Why Ray, you're a married

man with children.' My first reaction was to start explaining that although I was married, my wife knew I was looking around and she didn't mind. Suddenly I felt stupid standing there in the hallway telling a girl from the office all about my marital problems. I just dropped the subject and politely excused myself.

"Shortly after trying to date Marie, I met Diana, an executive secretary in the adjacent office. Diana was really nice, intelligent, well dressed, and somebody I could talk to. We had about four dates, and I thought I had really lucked out. On the fourth date we went to bed at her place, and I felt great. I called her a week later. She hit me with a bombshell. 'Ray, I'm sorry I can't see you anymore. A fellow who really loves me called and wants to start seeing me again. He and I could get serious. I know that you're only using me until you straighten things out with your wife. What's the use of continuing a relationship that has no future?'

"Quite discouraged, I didn't even look for anybody else to date for a few weeks. I wrote down the names of every possible single girl I knew. After fifteen minutes of scratching my head, I realized that I needed a new source of supply. I had no leads. This prompted me to try the bar scene. I knew that meeting people in bars was becoming quite popular.

"I must have been in that damn bar for two and one half hours before I even got a conversation going with a girl. All I seemed to encounter were stupid comments and blank stares. By midnight I was almost drunk from about eight scotch and waters. In disgust, I started to leave; then I met Eva.

"Eva was fortyish with blonde hair and black eyebrows. She was short and well built and flashily dressed. I figured there might be some action there. I bought her a drink and then she asked me if I had any 'stuff' on me. I was so naive, I thought she was referring to condoms, not drugs. Later she told me she was working for the Narcotics Bureau and was checking to see if I was pushing drugs. At that point I began to think she was weird, but my luck had been so bad, I was willing to try anything. She told me she had to get back to her children that night, but that she would really enjoy my companionship in the future. Eva told me not to call her because she and the children were staying with her mother. They had been evicted from their own apartment.

"Eva called me at the office the following Monday. We agreed to meet for dinner. After dinner and a few drinks we rented a room in a third-rate hotel in the downtown area. By one a.m. I had enough sex with Eva, so I told her that I would be leaving. She began to weep and talk about how lonely she was, and that I couldn't just get up and leave after such wonderful love-making. I felt sorry for her, so we stayed in bed and chatted until three in the morning. On the way home, I figured I would be better off not getting further involved with Eva.

"About ten days later Eva called me at the office and began weeping. She told me that now her mother was asking her and the children to leave the house. She also whimpered something about losing her job as a narcotics agent. I kept on telling her I was sorry to hear that things were going so poorly for her, and that maybe tomorrow would be better. Finally, she threatened to commit suicide if I didn't see her that night. I agreed to see her. She never showed up and fortunately she never called again.

"After awhile I began to think that I should

start at the top and work my way down again. Eva was absolute rock bottom. I called a really sharp girl who had been a client of mine. I felt uncomfortable about asking a customer for a date, so when I called I first talked about business. I told her about a new issue that might represent a good long range investment. Toward the end of our phone conversation, I suggested that we get together for a drink. She replied, 'I do not care to be hustled for business and pleasure at the same time. Perhaps I might report you to the Securities Exchange Commission.'

"All I could do at that point was hang up. I was too discouraged to think about who to call next."

Eunice, the Socially Handicapped Professor

Eunice, a 43 year old divorcée, is a professor of political science at a college in Nashville, Tennessee. Recently moved to the south, Eunice spent seven years working on a Ph.D. in political science, in order to become an independent woman. Shortly after her divorce, Eunice and her three children moved to Nashville. Did this new independence and self-sufficiency carry along with it an exciting personal life? Hardly. Eunice explains her disheartening experiences.

"Yes, I'm bitter. Gradually I realized that I am a socially handicapped person. It is a handicap in this world for a woman to have a doctorate. Most men really do not want an intellectual equal, much less an intellectual superior. When I tell men I am a political science professor, they want no part of me. However, I see no reason to hide my credentials. I worked very hard to get them.

"My first real date since being divorced was with the chairman of the history department. Ben was in his early fifties; a virile and attractive man. His divorce was pending and I saw him as a real possibility for myself. I figured he would dislike all those helpless female routines, so I made sure that I appeared professional and self-sufficient.

"Our professional interests were compatible. We both had extensive information about current events and recent history. I challenged his thinking and he challenged mine. He offered to buy me a nightgown. I thought he might be testing me out to see if I were frivolous, so I suggested instead that he get me a copy of *Civilisation* by Kenneth Clark.

"We had about ten dates over a two month period. One day I invited him to a department party. He said that he couldn't make it because of some other commitment, but that he would try and call me soon. Ben never called. He took up residence with a 21 year old senior home economics major.

"I was aghast at Ben's actions, but I chalked it off to a serious personality defect on his part. Our relationship probably would not have worked out if he could even entertain the notion of living with a girl young enough to be his daughter. Two months passed and nobody called me for a date. The holidays were approaching so I thought I had better get involved in some social life before I faced the depressing prospect of the holiday season without a man.

"My solution was to join a singles organization, 'The Nashville Sophisticates.' Women outnumbered men about two to one, but I didn't expect any more favorable odds. This time when I met a man I would not repeat the same mistake I made with Ben. I would find out before we even dated if he was seriously interested in meeting a mature, intelligent woman.

"The first man to ask me to dance at the club was a salesman for a company in town. He babbled on about how much he missed the fishing season, but he did seem like a sincere person. After buying me a drink, he asked, 'Say, honey, what do you do?' After learning that I was a professor of political science, he laughed and replied, 'Let me know when you run for President, I might vote for you.' He walked away without even asking for my telephone number.

"It then occurred to me to take the initiative in asking a man to dance who looked a little more intelligent. I spotted a quiet, sombre looking middle-aged man standing alone at the bar. After exchanging the usual pleasantries about the weather and the band at the club, he asked me if I were a secretary. I was indignant about his limited view of women. I answered, 'Indeed not, I hold a doctorate in political science.' In an angry voice, he muttered, 'What do you do, take care of sick politicians? We sure have a lot of them around.'

"Do you see what I mean when I say that being a highly educated woman is a social handicap?"

Marlene, Chet, Ingrid, Ray, and Eunice so far are all losers in the singles game. Instead of consistent sex, love, companionship and fun, they face loneliness. Each made a somewhat different mistake.

Marlene, the disgruntled teacher, is a chronic complainer. In her perception, her hometown was bad for meeting men, but so was New York City. To Marlene, men from Lancaster, Pennsylvania were provinical, but men from New York City were boorish. She concluded New York was a bad place to meet men after only scratching the surface of myriad possibilities. Marlene has a very limited view of the many maneuvers involved in the singles game.

She might have been more successful if she stayed with one approach long enough to find out if it could improve her social life. She could have made a systematic effort of getting to know other people in her building. Using this approach, Marlene might have been invited to parties where you can usually generate a few leads. Furthermore, why give up on computer dating after only one or two tries?

Chet, the uncool executive, is socially beating his head against a wall. Chet is betting on long shots and absorbing more than his share of rejection in the process. He keeps chasing after attractive young girls about half his age. Sure, Chet will score once in a while, but his chances for constant sex, love, companionship and fun are limited. If Chet continues in his present direction, in twelve years he will be sharing his pension and social security check with a chick (while she's making the scene with somebody more nearly her own age).

Chet so far is unwilling to play in his own league. Thousands of personable, interesting women in their late thirties or forties (all still at least ten years younger than he) would think Chet a good catch. Many of the young girls Chet chases think he is a dirty old man.

Ingrid, the isolated biochemist, is losing badly at the singles game because of her self-defeating rationalizations. She rationalizes that only the rural areas are safe places to raise children; that it is harmful for children to know that she has overnight male company. Ingrid is going to stay in her self-made solitary confinement until she takes some constructive action. Her life style—living in the country and going to sleep at ten—is ruining her chances to overcome her loneliness.

Were Ingrid not uncomfortable about being a social hermit, we wouldn't even be discussing her plight. But she wants to become a living, breathing, love-sharing, sex-experiencing woman. Until she sheds her self-imposed bind she will never achieve this happy status.

Ray, the married hunter, is taking rejection too seriously. As a married man living at home, Ray is at a disadvantage in finding an enduring relationship. In his present circumstances, many more women refuse than accept his offer because he is a high risk (he could very well never leave his wife). Ray is going to enjoy life much more when his knowledge of the singles game is as good as his knowledge of the stock market. Did Ray give up on stocks and bonds because at first he picked a few losers? No, he kept on prospecting for a winner and learned from his mistakes.

Eunice, the socially handicapped professor, might be creating her own social handicap. Whether she realizes it or not, Eunice is using her intellectual accomplishments as a weapon against men. Why does she have to hit men over the head with her Ph.D. in political science? Perhaps those jokesters Eunice encountered down in Nashville were in a small way returning her hostility by making put-down comments.

The title of Eunice's Ph.D. thesis was obviously not "An Unattached Person's Guide to Finding Sex, Love, Companionship, and Fun." If it were, she would be aware of a singles organization designed specifically to help intelligent, well educated, mature people find each other. (Read Chapter 12 and you will be better informed than Eunice about these matters).

How can you avoid singing the singles lament? How can you avoid some of the errors made by Marlene, Chet, Ingrid, Ray, and Eunice? How can you develop hundreds of positive strategies for playing the singles game? How can you have the right thing to say whenever you want to begin a conversation with an opposite-sexed stranger?

Read the rest of this book.

Chapter 2

THE TWELVE COMMANDMENTS

Success, in some degree, can be attained by almost everybody who plays the singles game. Few people are in such sad shape that they must forever lack companionship. Hundreds of specific suggestions for finding people are found later in this book. Follow the twelve general rules in this chapter and you are almost guaranteed to find and attract at least one opposite-sexed person. Many of the biggest losers in social life violate most of these twelve rules. Conversely, some of the biggest winners almost instinctively use these rules to play the singles game.

A word of caution. Merely because any one rule sounds obvious, do not overlook its importance. Obvious things can make the difference between success and failure in any activity. For instance, it is obvious that a tournament tennis player should think only of tennis while playing a match. Yet many top players have lost key matches precisely because their mind began to wander during a match.

1. *Shape Up Your Emotions*

Leave your major hang-ups home, or at least hide them, when searching for new relationships. Under the stress of loneliness, many people suffer from uncontrollable emotional bleeding. People who come into their webs, get spurted with bright red emotional blood. Diane is a case in point. She told a man on their first date: "Mike, there is something I must tell you. I could never fall in love with you because you look like my father. I hate my father because he rejected me when I was a child." If Mike had himself spent many hours in psychotherapy or sensitivity training, he might have thought, "This is good, she feels comfortable telling me her innermost feelings." Mike had neither of these experiences. Instead, he thought to himself, "I better drop this sick cookie right away before she flips."

Ivan, a would be swinger, is another example of how not to display your hang-ups early in a relationship. Louise, a woman he has escorted home from a singles club dance, is the recipient of this ultimatum: "Let us not play games. Either you and I spend the night together, or I will never see you again."

Mental health cannot be turned on and off with a switch. However, if you are turning off other people by uncalled for openness *too early in a relationship*, get professional help. Perhaps a psychiatrist, psychologist, or some other competent personal counselor can become the recipient of your innermost feelings about opposite-sexed persons. Encounter groups might also provide the opportunity you need to air your problems. Use a close friend as a confidante.

Shouldn't one be able to express feelings to a person of the opposite sex? Definitely yes; but only after the relationship has begun to solidify. Few people know how to handle total emotional honesty from a person they barely know. Many potentially good relationships have been ruined because a man or woman had the uncontrollable urge to mutter, "I love you" on the first or second date.

2. *Shape Up Your Intellect*

A giant-sized intellect is not required to play the singles game, but intellectually alert people make more interesting companions. After years of relating to only one person, a newly unattached person may not recognize the need for being an interesting conversationalist. Revamping your intellect is not as formidable as it sounds. Anyone but a mental defective can acquire some new information without suffering a mental hernia. I have two elementary, albeit useful, suggestions.

Suggestion number one is to beef up your fund of general information. Acquire a sparse amount of knowledge about a wide variety of topics. Thirty minutes per day of concentrated reading is all that is required for the person of average intelligence to accomplish this feat. Two hundred and ten minutes per week invested in reading newspapers or news magazines will keep you well informed.

Another way to acquire some knowledge about many different fields is to read book reviews. In addition to summarizing the strength and weaknesses of the book under review, a book review includes some general information about the topic.

Add some variety to your general knowledge. Read a speciality magazine such as *Ms.*, *Penthouse*, or the *National Enquirer*. Conversation lulls that occur when you are trying to turn on to another person will then be easy to handle. Tidbits of inside information can be inserted such as, "Have you heard about that woman scientist in Bavaria who had demonstrated that the female sex organ has 317 separate muscles and the male sex organ has only 273?" (Even if a few of your vital facts are incorrect, he or she probably will not have read the same article.)

Suggestion number two is to acquire intensive knowledge about one field. In the eyes of other people, this makes you an *expert*. Women find expertise sexy. Gradually, men are developing the same reaction to expertise in women. Uninformed women are losing their sex appeal, owing at least in part to women's lib.

Select a field for expertise that is relatively unique. Forget professional football. Twenty million Americans—many of whom have never even tossed a football in their backyards—are already capable Monday morning quarterbacks. Karen, a stocks and bonds salesperson, is a bug on older automobiles. She impresses dates by identifying the make and year of automobiles shown in old movies. "Look at the condition of that 1947 Lincoln Zephyr," said Karen to her boyfriend while they were lying in bed watching television.

3. *Shape Up Your Body*

Firm, solid bodies are in style. Shaping up your body will increase your attractiveness to a wide range of people. Few men or women have the basic body type or the time and energy required to resemble an Olympic swimmer; but almost anybody can improve his or her physique. Your goal should be physical fitness. Physical perfection isn't required to play the singles game.

Avoid the extremes of obesity or emaciation as a general guideline. "Overweight" and "underweight" mean different things to different people. However, few males will approach an obese female. And few females will date a grossly overweight male if given a choice. Extreme thinness can also lower your appeal to some people. Boney, gaunt people look much older than their actual years. Besides, flesh is much more fun to fondle than bones. High fashion models may be photogenic, but undressed they are breastless and hipless—two very unsexy female characteristics to many men. A boney chested, protruding ribbed male, girls tell me, is also short on sex appeal.

Work on bodily imperfections you can change through proper exercise and diet. Cast aside concerns about your height, the length of your legs, or the size of your head. Take constructive action on changeable aspects of your physique.

A combination of proper diet and exercise can improve the physical appearance of almost anybody. All diet and exercise programs work on the same principle. Weight loss is inevitable if you consume less food yet burn more energy.

Formal programs of body building or weight-reducing exercises are good. A fringe benefit is that you might meet people while jogging, attending Take Off Pounds Sensibly (TOPS), or visiting a health spa. Body building can also take place in the context of daily living. Get in some extra walking by parking your car in the most remote area of the lot. Run down the hall with your garbage. Avoid elevator rides when you can walk up the stairs. Jog to the mail box. Squeeze a tennis ball while riding the subway or when waiting for traffic lights in your car.

Make sexual intercourse part of your daily living. Recent research has revealed that sexercise can be good for your heart and muscles.

4. *Check Out Your Plumage*

Human males, like peacocks, display their best plumage when on the make, according to a study conducted by a sociologist. Females looking for new male companionship also upgrade their wardrobes. Fancy plumage may not be necessary to attract opposite sexed people, but at least make sure that your attire is not hindering your chances of finding sex, love, or companionship.

A careful look at your wardrobe may indicate

that much of your clothing is soup stained or no longer stylish. Take action and fit some new clothing into your budget. Get the best social return on your investment by following a few common sense suggestions.

Avoid the "I just stepped out of a clothing store" look. People who wear everything new create the impression that they are dissatisfied with their old selves—or even worse—that they just returned from a long incarceration. Phasing into a wardrobe can also help you avoid the "Wow, who are your trying to impress" reactions from friends.

Select new clothing that is appropriate to your age and life circumstances. Gary, a divorced foreman, bought a new wardrobe befitting a chairman of the board, down to a long black umbrella and homburg. Peggy, a newly separated copy editor, age 39, outfitted herself with selections from the Junior Miss Shop. Both Gary and Peggy look pretentious and foolish.

Clothing you choose to increase your attractiveness should befit your self-image. Select attire that you feel comfortable wearing because it reflects your real personality—not an image that somebody else thinks you should project.

Ted was left by his girlfriend of five years. Among other things, she objected to his conservative nature. Overcompensating, Ted dressed garishly. Not only did he look foolish, he felt foolish. His talk and actions were conservative, yet his wardrobe was flamboyant. The discrepancy between Ted's personality and his style of dress was self-defeating. Conservative girls—those best suited for Ted—thought he looked immature. Less conservative girls were attracted to Ted on first impression, but they quickly realized that his clothing was deceiving.

5. *Make Up Your Own Definition of Attractive*

Liberate yourself from cultural stereotypes about what makes for an attractive person. Go after people *you* consider attractive. Somebody sharp is somebody that fits your personal description of a good mate.

Mildred, a tall, intelligent assertive woman, prefers short, less assertive men. Her last two boyfriends earn less money than she does. Great for Mildred. She is happy and so are her boyfriends.

Ed pursues girls most men would describe as unattractive. Ed, himself attractive, reasons this way. "Girls that other people consider beautiful are hard to live with. They play that prima donna routine that I won't tolerate. My girlfriend wouldn't make the centerfold in *Playboy*. I consider that her strength. She's a sharp cookie and a real person."

6. *Play In Your Own League*

Terry, a single 26 year old computer operator, is five feet six, a high school graduate and commands an above average income. Terry only wants to get involved with tall jet setters. He saves his vacation dollar for trips to the finest ski resorts in his quest for long stemmed, statuesque women. At home, he cavorts in the poshest singles bar, hoping to make it with his version of an ideal woman. Terry's batting average is terrible. Rarely does he encounter tall, sophisticated women willing to date him. All Terry has to show for his relationships with tall jet setters so far is some cancelled checks and a few disappointing evenings.

Maxine, a separated 43 year old elementary school teacher, is attractive and has three teenage children. She seeks a divorced man her age or younger to move in with her and the children.

Maxine's physical attractiveness, combined with her other good qualities, has brought her a few exciting affairs with men in her preferred age range. Yet all three of these romances came to the same crunching halt. Bill, Jim, and Larry fled when it became apparent that Maxine was looking for a merger. All were willing sometime companions and lovers. But the prospects of total immersion into Maxine's family unit triggered their panic buttons. Maxine was left to search for another replacement.

Terry and Maxine made the same strategic error in playing the singles game. Both tried to play outside their own league. Terry, if behaving rationally, would prospect for shorter girls with less glamorous life styles. Maxine could also be more realistic. A 43 year old divorcée with three children has a very small chance of attracting and keeping a man her age or younger. Maxine would be less disappointed if she prospected for men ten years older than herself. Many 53 year old men would welcome the chance to date a younger, intelligent woman like Maxine.

Few people, males or females, would be considered a big catch by every other available opposite-sexed person. The truth is that only a fairly limited range of people would be interested in buying what you have to sell. Figure out who these people are and go after them; they are your real prospects.

Mary is a 31 year old attorney, single and physically well proportioned. On paper she has terrific credentials for attracting men. She is accomplished, intelligent, attractive and earns a handsome income. Yet the number of available men in her league is actually quite limited. Mary needs a mature, intelligent male who is secure enough to handle a bright and accomplished gal.

Brad, a 26 year old escapee from the suburbs, is a hippie type who works as a computer programmer. His work hours are irregular and so are his dating habits. Brad's idea of a big time with a girl is to buy a bottle of cheap wine, listen to his stereo collection, and ball on a mattress laid out on the floor of his studio apartment. Some girls think Brad has a lot to offer (he's a genuine person not hung up with traditional middle class standards). But Brad does best when he confines his woman hunting to a narrow circle of women. Girls Brad meet at work think he is weird and cheap.

Sometimes it pays to play in a less competitive league. Assume that you are re-entering the singles market after a long involvement with one person. Perhaps you have been prospecting for companionship, but your luck has been poor. Try lowering your standards for awhile until you regain your self-confidence. Make somebody who you wouldn't date if your social life were going well happy.

Nick, a man of many romances, is a strong advocate of playing in a lesser league between heavy relationships. "I am never between chicks for long. I can't take waiting around for a perfect romance. When I've split with a sharp woman, I look for some action to tide me over until the next sharp one." I don't scrape the barrel or use prostitutes, but I become a little less fussy. For a two month period I was balling a girl I didn't consider at all bright. But she wasn't half bad."

"But Nick," I asked him, "Do you feel that you are taking advantage of these women you date between more serious involvements?" "Not at all," replied Nick, "I never tell them I love them or that it's going to last."

A final note about choosing your league. Many people have made it outside their own league; give it a try if you want. Remember, I'm talking about increasing your chances of success, and decreasing your chances of failure. If you are adventuresome take an occasional chance on a long shot.

7. *Calculate Your Odds*

Be realistic in your search for a compatible mate. Astronomical are the odds against finding a person who meets *all* of your specifications. Roughly, here is how it works. Nancy wants to meet a man; one out of two people are male. Nancy wants a Catholic male; one out of four people are Catholic. Nancy wants a male between ages 25 and 30; about one out of seven people are in this age bracket. Nancy wants a man making over twenty-seven thousand dollars per year; one out of a hundred people make this much money. Nancy wants a college graduate; one out of five males have a college degree or better. Nancy wants her man to be single; about one out of six males are single. Nancy wants a man at least average in appearance; about one out of two men fit this requirement.

Where does that astronomical figure come from? Nancy's chances of finding a single Catholic male between the age of 25 and 30, making over 27 thousand dollars who is also attractive are one in 10,040,000. About twenty people in the United States fit Nancy's exact description of a satisfactory mate. By being a little less fussy, Nancy can dramatically increase her chances. If she drops the religious requirement and drops the acceptable income down to fifteen thousand per year, about one person in 50,000 will meet her requirements.

Obviously, my statistics are not exact; a precise

answer to Nancy's chances would take two years to find, but the general idea is correct. Every characteristic you require in a prospective lover multiplies your chances of never finding that person. If only one out of ten women are natural blondes, and you insist on finding a natural blonde, you have made it ten times more difficult to find a mate. If you insist on finding a man over 5′9″ tall, you have doubled your chances of not finding a man.

Before embarking upon your great people hunt, think carefully about dropping off one or two of your rigid requirements. Why bet on the longest shot in the race? Girls, does that prospect really have to have an IQ over 125, play a musical instrument, enjoy pets, not enjoy professional football, and have a nine inch sex organ? Fellows, does your prospective mate have to have less formal education than you, be under 5′8″ tall, have no children, and achieve orgasm nine out of ten times?

Already I can hear the protests from my readers. Statistical information says nothing about love, personal attraction, or *chemistry*. Considerations of this nature are so crucial I have saved them for last. Aside from all those measurable characteristics mentioned above, everybody wants to meet someone with whom he or she has good chemistry. Finding the right statistical fit may increase the chances of good chemistry, but that *certain feeling* has to be there to make life fun.

On the average, it takes about twenty carefully chosen dates with different people before you find a genuine chemical reaction. Carefully chosen means that you exercise discretion in asking for or accepting dates. Your twentieth date is unlikely to produce a giant chemical reaction if you date just any nineteen people you meet. Consider yourself lucky if you find good mutual chemistry with a handful of people in your lifetime. Don't put so many restrictions on the type of people you will consent to date that body and mind chemistry never has a chance to surface.

8. *Place Yourself in a Favorable Light*

Projecting an image of realistic self-confidence increases your ability to attract opposite-sexed persons. People feel the most confident—and appear the most confident—when they are doing something that places them in a favorable light. A male jockey may not have the best woman-drawing power while strolling on the beach, but back at the track he's dynamite with certain women. Placed in the winner's circle, a jockey finds many women who just *adore* short men. A slight of build singer strolling in the park is just another person. On stage she is a petite femme fatale who men are eager to meet.

Ideally, meet people while doing something you do well. Be it a hobby, job, or community service, you are the most attractive to other people when you look confident and natural. When you are in control of what you are doing, you are on your way toward being in charge of a promising social situation. Golf, tennis, and ski instructors (of both sexes) owe part of their sex success to this principle.

What should you do when there are limited opportunities to meet people while doing what you do best? Maybe you install telephone poles, fight forest fires, nurse the aged, or fish for tuna for a living. Maybe your hobby is stamp collecting, crocheting, ice fishing, or hunting. What are some ways in which a person might project a favorable image outside of his or her natural habitat? A few illustrations may help you.

Paul, a worshipper of sun and attractive females, does most of his prospecting on the beach. Paul's success ratio hit its zenith when he switched radios. In the past, average-appearing Paul would ask females to join him for some radio listening. Paul would point sheepishly to his small AM-FM radio receiver as he extended the invitation. Paul placed himself in an unfavorable situation. He appeared foolish extending such a mundane invitation. Paul got wise. He invested in a large black AM-FM plus short wave receiver with a giant antenna.

Now he had something unusual to offer which made his invitation attractive and put him in a more favorable light. After a few moments of small talk, Paul would go into this routine, "By the way, you're welcome to listen to my short wave radio with me. I think I might be getting some authentic Austrian folk music soon.

Warren is a busy man. Neither his job as a civil engineer or his hobby as a gun collector brings him into contact with many women. Warren chose computer dating as a source of women. At first he fumbled badly on the phone. "You are probably wondering if there is something wrong with me for having to use a computer dating service. There really isn't anything wrong with me. I just don't like the normal way of meeting people." Warren placed himself in such an unfavorable light with this routine that his relationships were doomed from the start.

Warren changed his opening tactics. "Hello, this is Warren Burns. I was given your name through Computer Dating. It sounds like a sensible way to meet compatible people. Would you like to give getting together a try." Projecting this healthy degree of self-confidence, Warren started his computer dates off on a better footing.

Sandy wanted to meet important men, but as a secretary in a television studio she felt she lacked the status necessary to attract important men. Sandy wanted to appear confident and important in her own right to important people. Sly Sandy had an inspired idea. She begged to become the assistant to the program director of a morning talk show. Here is how she worked her plan.

Sandy asked permission to label her job "guest coordinator." She took on the responsibility of telephoning potential guests for the show. Sandy even made suggestions to her boss about what local celebrities the show should try to attract. Sandy now had license to call almost any important man she wanted.

"How do you do Mr. —————. This is Sandy Thomas from the Early Morning Show on WVBN, Channel 14. My assignment as guest coordinator is to contact prospective guests for our show. Your name has been mentioned as a person with a potential contribution to make to our programming effort . . ."

As you would expect, many male guests who appeared on the show were interested in meeting that alert program coordinator. Sandy is now married to a high-ranking city official in her town government who once appeared on the Early Morning Show.

9. *Avoid Desperate Tactics*

Desperate tactics send out vibrations that frighten away some good prospects. As irresistible as your new prospect or date might be, keep the lid on self-defeating acts of desperation. Let us look at some desperate tactics in action.

Brenda, an adorable but insecure woman of 29, is an unwitting master of the most common desperate tactic, *premature mention of marriage*. Brenda's preoccupation with marriage sends out a message to her dates that she is in hot pursuit of a husband. During dinner with Gerry, a man she had known for two weeks, Brenda described the relative merits of marriage versus living with a man. "I would never live with a man. If he left me, I couldn't collect alimony."

Arden displayed a desperate tactic to his new girlfriend by talking about marriage before he talked about love. After three weeks of dating Charlene, Arden proposed marriage. He explained how Charlene met all his requirements for a wife and how happy he would be if they were married. Charlene retorted, "Fine for you Arden, but what about my feelings? What would our marriage do for me? You haven't even told me that you love me and you don't really even know me as a person. How could you possibly know that I'm the right woman for you?"

Roger, much to his chagrin, has aborted three promising relationships in one year. His desperate tactic is called the *multiple date blitz*. Roger's actions with Sue are a good example of how his blitz works. Roger calls Sue, a girl he recently met at a party, to request a date for the following Saturday night. Sue replies with an encouraging "Yes, that would be nice." Desperate Roger can't leave well enough alone and allow his relationship with Sue to develop gradually. He moves in with the *multiple date blitz:*

"Sue, while I have you on the phone, there is something else I want to ask you. Would you like to get together for a drink this Tuesday night? But even more important, I want to take you to the park on Sunday afternoon."

Sue suddenly felt messages of desperation coming through the telephone receiver. "What is this guy Roger trying to pull? I don't even know him and he has asked me out for three dates." Predictably, Sue was non-committal about Tuesday and Sunday. Saturday night she was on guard for any other signs of unusual behavior on Roger's part, thus starting the relationship off on a negative note.

Sylvia frightens off men she likes with the *long range blitz.* Sylvia very much wants to form a lasting relationship with a man. When she begins dating a man she wants for a lasting relationship, she takes steps to schedule some future get-togethers. For instance, she began dating Phil around Labor Day. After their third date Sylvia asked Phil to escort her to an annual Halloween party given by her club. Phil weakly consented, noting that Halloween was almost two months away. October 1, Sylvia invited Phil to a dinner dance given by her company early in December. Phil fled with the parting comment, "Really Sylvia, I don't want to be tied down to one relationship at this point."

Jack suffers from *premature ejaculation of love words,* a desperate tactic that has cost him more than one potentially good relationship. After one or two dates with any girl he finds attractive, Jack has the uncontrollable urge to whisper, "I love you." Among the put-downs he has received in response to his enthusiasm are, "You must be kidding," "Could you possibly mean that?" and "You seem like a nice fellow but you're rushing things."

Bill uses a common desperate tactic—one that has given him the reputation of a pest. Bill will not gracefully accept rejection. Women have to clobber him with, "No, I don't want to see you," before he politely goes away. Joyce, after dating him twice, declined thirteen subsequent social invitations extended by Bill. Joan gave Bill the excuse that she was busy for the next seventeen nights. In hot pursuit, Bill phoned eighteen days later, stating, "I guess we can finally get together tonight."

10. *Soft Pedal Past Relationships*

An almost guaranteed method of cooling down a brand new relationship is to compare that person to past lovers. Some allusion to your past social life is inevitable, but a persistence on this theme annoys most people, *whether or not they admit it.*

Enid unwittingly alienates new men in her life by constant reference to past romances. Her references to past affairs before she and a new boyfriend have even bedded down are devastating. "Pete and I had a fantastic love affair that we carried out in two countries. What a great summer that was for the both of us," she told Barry, who retorted, "Very fine for Pete, but it bugs the hell out of me to hear about a guy you've shacked up with when I've hardly kissed you good-night."

Comparing the sexual performance of present to past lovers only adds to a relationship when your new lover is given a more favorable rating. An important strategy is to make *absolute,* not *relative,* comparisons. In other words, "You are a magnificent lover," is safer than, "You are a better lover than practically all the other men in my life." And, "What an explosive orgasm," will win you more points than, "Even my wife didn't have an orgasm that good."

Bragging about the calibre of people you dated in the past is a subtle put-down. An inference often drawn by the person you are now cultivating is that things were better for you in the past. "Tom and I went to the nicest places," is an effective way of making your new man feel he *isn't* taking you to the nicest places.

Complaining about former lovers can also hamper a new relationship. Astute dates will interpret such complaints as a tip-off that you are still emotionally involved with a past romance. Judy tells new boyfriends all about the misery of her first marriage. Ron describes how Judy turned him off:

"You would have thought I was Judy's old husband and she was chewing me out. She went over in intimate detail how Henry, her ex-husband, had sexual relations with her sister. Also, she never let up on how bad that guy was to the kids. One Christmas he was too drunk to put the kids toys together. I told Judy to go tell her problems to somebody else. I wanted somebody interested in me, not in talking about somebody from the past."

11. *Combat Loneliness*

Loneliness is the unattached person's natural enemy. Loneliness can make you depressed, give you ulcers, rob you of sleep, cause you to oversleep, provoke you into over-eating, or make you look toward drugs as a solution to your problem. If those consequences aren't bad enough, loneliness can also encourage you to grab onto any relationship, however superficial or destructive. Loneliness can even take the fun out of playing the singles game.

Loneliness stemming from neurotic conflicts is best dealt with in psychotherapy. Loneliness stemming from an impoverished relationship with God is best dealt with by religious experience. Loneliness stemming from not having an opposite-sexed friend whose company you enjoy can be conquered. The four suggestions I describe next are a good starting point.

Loneliness based on not having a lover or mate can only be cured by finding a lover or mate. Every other solution is superficial, temporary, or even absurd in comparison to finding a living, breathing, communicating human. Combating loneliness by raising goldfish, for example, is about as effective as combating overweight by purchasing larger sized clothing. If you are convinced that the best antidote to loneliness is finding somebody, act upon some of the suggestions throughout this book.

Loneliness is often less noticeable and painful when you concentrate some effort on helping a needy person. Do something nice for somebody lonelier, more depressed, poorer, and less fortunate than yourself. Spend some time at the county infirmary reading the newspaper to an aged blind person. Bring a skid row derelict home with you for Thanksgiving weekend and buy him a new overcoat. Buy a poor child a brand new tricycle. Even the most hardened, embittered, self-centered reader of this book will feel better (and less lonely) if he or she follows through on one of these simple acts of kindness.

Pamper yourself between affairs; perhaps your loneliness will feel a little less acute. What about buying yourself a new shirt or sweater with the money you save by not going out Saturday night? Wax your car, clean your closets, buy a painting, get your camera overhauled, shop for a new dress, or have your ears pierced. Pampering yourself may not be as constructive as finding a mate or helping a less fortunate person, but it does help a needy cause—you in your present predicament.

Finally, if lonely and unattached ponder some of your advantages. Reflect upon how many of your friends are unhappily married. Realize that the next opposite sexed person who has dinner with you will do so out of choice, not out of obligation or necessity. Bask in the envy that so many married people have for the glamorous world of the single adult. Should these rationalizations fail, try this philosophy volunteered by Perry, an unattached male: "Not knowing where my next sex partner is coming from is a drag, but it beats knowing who my *last* sex partner is."

12. *Keep On Prospecting*

Maybe your next romance will be your prince or princess charming. Maybe you and that person satisfy each other forever. Maybe nothing catastrophic will happen to that dream person. Realistically, the odds are high that you will be back playing the singles game. Plan ahead. Never stop prospecting. Keep your eyes open for someone who could become your next lover if you and your present lover ever split.

Callous? No, realistic. I am not advocating that you conduct a formal campaign to find a replacement for somebody that you love today. But do not terminate social contacts simply because you do not need them now. Continue to widen your sphere of friends and acquaintances. Continue to cultivate platonic friends of the opposite sex. Attend parties where both couples and singles are invited. Don't be rude to people who ask you for a date. You never know when that innocent conversation over coffee will result in next year's lover.

Chapter 3

OPENING THE RELATIONSHIP

Every human relationship begins with a conversation between two people. "What do you say for openers?" is a question facing anybody in search of a new date or mate. You need an opening line even for a one-time sexual encounter. Nobody has sexual intercourse without first communicating or conversing with another person. People unable to talk (deaf mutes, for example) use sign language or lip movements to pick up prospective dates or lovers. Should both you and your prospective partner each speak a different language, communication will take place by facial gestures and eye contact. In short, anybody seeking sex, love, companionship, or fun needs to develop some skill in engaging other people—often absolute strangers —in conversation.

This chapter provides you with eleven guidelines and over seventy sample opening lines for beginning conversation with a stranger of the opposite sex. Included also are about two dozen opening lines to avoid. It is important that you first understand the general principles before using the sample opening lines. Once you master the general principles, with a little imagination you will be able to develop some opening lines of your own to suit almost any occasion.

General Principles

1. *Males and females can take the initiative in starting a conversation.* Despite women's liberation, many people still feel that men have to make the first move in any relationship. Untrue.

Men are flattered and pleasantly surprised when a woman they consider attractive (or even presentable) takes the first step in starting a conversation. Most men have underlying concerns about being rejected by a prospect. When a woman takes the initiative in starting the conversation, it serves as an indicator: "Wow, she must find me attractive or O.K." Men who are hung up about a sharp difference between male and female roles may not know how to handle an approach by a woman. Women, however, must not overlook two important points. First, unless you trip over that man you think is appealing, he may not see you and a relationship will never get started. Second, men who are hung up about male versus female roles may not be the best prospects for you.

2. *Ask open-ended questions*. This hint stems from any experienced interviewer's notebook. Questions that can be answered categorically (for example, "yes" or "no") are conversation stoppers. Open-ended questions—those that require an explanation from another person—are conversation openers. Assume that a woman eyes an appealing man sitting on a bench at a public tennis court. She wants to make contact. Observe the difference in results between asking a categorical versus an open-ended question.

Categorical:
She: Is that your steel tennis racket?
He: Yes.

Open-ended:
She: What effect has using a steel racket had upon your game?
He: Well, at first I thought I was playing with a trampoline and then I began to notice that I was actually . . . (He proceeds into a five minute monologue which

leads to a twenty minute dialogue and starts what could be a beautiful relationship.)

Next, our attention focuses on a much less romantic setting—a singles bar. A man spots a woman he would like to pursue.

Categorical:

He: Do you like the music here?

She: No.

Open-ended:

He: What do you think of the group?

She: The music is good, but I think they should play some slower numbers. That way more old-fashioned people could dance . . . (This will give the man plenty of opportunity to proceed further with the conversation. He can simply react to some of her statements.)

3. *Appear honest and sincere.* Women are leery of men who try to pick them up by fabricating stories about themselves. Singles bars and resorts are densely populated by males (and some females) who glorify their real occupation or distort other important facts about themselves. Even if an insincere, fabricated statement about yourself does open a conversation, it may well backfire after the truth is discovered. It is difficult to hide your real job (or lack of one) and marital status after one or two dates. Here are some opening lines that immediately arouse suspicions of insincerity or actual dishonesty:

"I'm Bill Durand, an executive from IBM." (The man is about age 23 in appearance. No IBM executives are that young! Besides, an executive would not call himself one. More probably he would say something like, "I'm the financial vice president at _____."

"I just learned today that my wife will spend the rest of her life in a mental hospital." (If this were true, he should be home making arrangements for her hospital stay, not hanging out in a bar, museum, or other public place.)

"May I sit down next to you? I wrenched my knee today in the giant slalom olympic trials." (If he were indeed an olympic skier, he wouldn't have to be out hustling women!)

"I'm a starlet and you look familiar." (If she were really a starlet she would probably be well provided for by an affluent movie producer. Worse, if she thinks she is a starlet, she may expect you to lavish her with entertainment and gifts.)

In contrast to these hackneyed lines, here is a highly effective conversation opener that exudes sincerity (particularly if you mean it):

"You look like a nice person. Could you tell me who you are?"

4. *Fumble just a little.* Earlier in this book I talked about the importance of projecting a confident image. True, but there is a fine line between self-confidence and being super-cool, or over-rehearsed and over-experienced. An opening line, to be effective, should not seem to have been used one hundred times before. "Sweetheart, I like your style," is one such super-cool statement. Whipping out a gold-plated, butane cigarette lighter is another cliché that projects the image of an experienced pick-up artist.

Girls have told me it is particularly effective if the man who fumbles a little, nevertheless looks like someone experienced in meeting women. Next are two illustrations of the "fumble a little principle" that led to two very warm romances for an acquaintance of mine:

He, to a sexy, young attractive girl sitting in a

hotel lobby where the Daughters of the American Revolution were holding a convention:

"By any chance, do you belong to the DAR?" Although this is a categorical question, predictably the girl burst into laughter and the first step in a worthwhile relationship began.

He, to a woman contemplating a painting in an art gallery:

"I'm embarrassed about asking a total stranger this question, but what is the difference between a modern and a contemporary painting?" My acquaintance's planned fumble worked beautifully. She picked up the ball and they are now living together.

5. *Don't put people on the defensive.* One method of preventing a relationship from beginning is to put your prospect on the defensive. You are then more likely to be involved in an argument than in the start of a potentially meaningful relationship. One quick way of putting another person on the defensive is to make them feel uncomfortable about being in their present situation. The question, "Why does a good-looking person like you have to resort to a lonely hearts club?" is almost guaranteed to make somebody defensive. "How many computer dates have you had, anyway?" is another uncomfortable question. "Why are you divorced, (separated, unattached, etc.)" is also good for extinguishing any potential sparks of rapport.

Unless you are a private detective or an FBI agent on a secret mission, don't conduct an interrogation. Defensiveness and constricted conversation is almost inevitable under these circumstances. Here is an unwitting interrogation conducted by a woman three minutes after she had met a man at a party:

"Where do you work? What is your job? How old are you? Do you live with your mother? Do you go to church or temple?"

Our interrogator probably felt she was only looking for topics of conversation, but her line of questioning comes across as an investigation of his credentials. After several direct questions of this nature, your prospect may question your right to ask such questions.

6. *Make a relevant or clever observation.* Making a comment that fits the logic of the situation is an effective conversation opener. Try to avoid being trite. For instance, assume you are standing on a street corner in Washington D.C. during a July heat wave. You spot a woman you find appealing. Don't say, "Hot today, isn't it?" Try also to avoid making an observation so technical or obscure in meaning that your prospect will be at a loss for a reaction. Suppose you are trying to initiate contact with a girl on the beach. You might be blocking off potential conversation if you try this opening line: "I think this shell is from the paleozoic era."

What is a relevant or clever comment? Imagine that you are seated next to a prospect in an airplane that has yet to take off. You might say, "It looks like a forty-five minute delay on the ground." Should you be in a San Juan casino, you might comment to a prospect, "It looks like the fifty dollar chips are moving faster than the five dollar chips."

7. *Appeal to a person's intellect and talents, not just to his or her physical characteristics.* One unfortunate aspect of most first encounters is that people seek out other people mostly on the basis of superficial characteristics. If you direct your opening line toward other aspects of that person,

you could be at a distinct advantage. Imagine how frequently a 6'7" male has heard girls say to him, "Gosh, you are tall." Girls with bust size forty-two tire of hearing upon first encounter, "My, that's a nice blouse you are wearing," (which really means, "I would love to get my hands on those large breasts of yours.") Commenting favorably upon another person's clothes may be flattering to most people, but it is less personal than a comment about their talent or skill.

Appeals can readily be made to another person's intellect or talents if you first do a little homework about that person. You must also know who your prospect is and where he or she can be seen again. Next are some sincere approaches that illustrate the principle of appealing to another person's intellect or talent:

"I was so impressed with that presentation you gave in class last night about ecology. May I ask you a few questions?"

"I heard that you just won an award in the plant for your suggestion about safety. Congratulations."

"It's too bad you didn't win the Sale's Executive Club beauty contest. but I don't think that is very important. Those comments you made were so convincing and so well put."

"A mutual friend told me that you are the absolute authority on Japanese art in this building. May I pick your brain over a sukiyaki dinner this Thursday?"

"May I make an appointment to come to your office, Professor Farber? I'd like to talk about having you as an advisor for a special studies project. I thought my course with you was terrific."

8. *Share a common experience.* Many pick-ups have to be executed in a hurry. One man spotted a

girl on the street who was moving hurriedly away from a derelict. She hopped on a bus to avoid her pursuer. The younger man then hopped on the bus in pursuit of her and initiated a conversation with this opening line: "Was that poor old man bothering you, too? He asked me for some money. What do you think should be done to help such people?" A unique conversation had begun in a way that did not seem contrived. The derelict had provided the opportunity for sharing a common experience. In short, keep on your mental toes to find some experience that you and your prospect have shared or are about to share. Here are some opening lines that could be the first step toward a good relationship:

Male to female in movie lobby: "What did you think of that ending?"

Female to male on line at an airport: "What do you think are the prospects that you and I will get bumped from this flight?"

Male to female at blood bank: "Do I appear as white as you do? Is there any chance they took too much blood from us?"

Male to female on street corner waiting for bus: "I guess the bus system has broken down again. What do you think the city should do to improve service?" (If he receives any conversational spark, the man might invite the girl to share a taxi ride with him to her destination.)

9. *Touch your prospect at the earliest opportunity.* Touching is in style. Done with sensitivity, and at the right place on the body, touching can provide an instant spark to a relationship. Women are at a distinct advantage in this realm. When a man touches a woman, it can simply communicate his interest in entering into a physical relationship. When a woman touches a man, it connotes a

special interest in getting close to him, both physically and emotionally. Women are more selective in their touching. Almost no man will walk away from a woman at a party who gives him the slightest touch with her hand. It conveys tenderness, warmth, and an ever-so-mild tinge of seductiveness. Touching a woman's arm, running a finger down her cheek, or grasping her hand can be effective approaches to getting a relationship started. In spite of the sexual revolution, grabbing a woman's buttocks or brushing against her breasts upon initial encounters are often relationship killers.

10. *Don't undress her with your eyes.* Many men first stare at a prospect before engaging her in conversation. Staring is usually an indication that the male is contemplating how the woman looks naked. Women can sense this and it makes them feel uncomfortable. Women appreciate admiring glances, not penetrating stares. Girls have also mentioned that prolonged stares suggest that the man staring might be mentally ill.

Making a stranger feel uncomfortable by staring is self-defeating. She is likely to reject striking up a converation with you. Women, in contrast, can stare all they want. Men enjoy being stared at by female strangers.

11. *Don't take rejection personally.* Nobody, man or woman, scores all the time or even most of the time in picking up strangers. Even the most attractive, self-confident men have more failures than successes in playing the singles game. Probably one hundred reasons exist why one person may reject another upon initial contact. That interesting looking young man you approached coming off the golf course may be preoccupied with a clumsy putt he just executed. That adorable girl

you just eyed on the bus may be deep in thought about an upcoming audition for a lead in a play. Furthermore, just because a stranger is standing alone it does not mean that he or she is unattached, or attached and looking for an affair.

Don't take rejection personally even if nine out of ten prospects refuse to consider getting together with you for a second meeting. All you need is one acceptance to turn a pedestrian personal life into an exciting adventure.

A Potpourri of Opening Lines

Practically all of the opening lines offered next follow one of the eleven general principles. Some violate the principle of asking open-ended questions. You will encounter situations when a categorical question is the only one that seems appropriate. Many of these conversation openers can be used anywhere. Certain others are only suited to special circumstances. Common sense, and a few hints from me, will enable you to make the necessary distinction. Many of these conversation openers are equally suited for males or females; others will produce better results when used by one sex. You will be able to tell the difference from their wording. My opening lines are numbered for convenience.

1. Hello. (This is a fantastic opening line. I wish I could take credit for it. Probably millions of relationships between men and women have begun on this basis. If you feel more comfortable with "Hi", the results will be equally good.

2. Hello, what is your name? (Another highly effective conversation opener. It immediately places the focus on the person you are trying to cultivate and not upon you.)

3. Hello, my name is _____. (Almost as

effective as asking another person his or her name. Once a person knows your name, you are no longer an anonymous stranger.)

4. Well, hello. (Females can use this line with incredibly good results. It is warm, friendly, and tinged with sensuality all at the same time. One speech therapist I know began several exciting relationships with this pleasant opener.)

5. Hi, my name is _____. Tell me about yourself. (This opener is double barrelled. First you identify yourself, thus lowering the suspicion of talking to an absolute stranger. Second, you give your prospect a good opportunity to start talking about something very familiar—himself or herself.) Caution: Inarticulate or unsophisticated people find the statement, "Tell me about yourself", difficult to handle.

6. Good evening. (I would rate this line only passable and certainly very uncreative. However, you might keep this as a standby in case nothing more appropriate comes to mind in a given situation.)

7. I'm having a difference of opinion with a friend of mine. He thinks you are a secretary and I think you are a lawyer. Could you help me settle this argument? (Although complex, this line shows that you do not have a sexist view of the world and that you think she is intelligent looking. Both aspects put you in a favorable light with a modern woman.)

8. You look like somebody carrying out an important mission. (Any girl who uses this opener in a hotel, airplane, train, or even a street corner is almost guaranteed of meeting a new man.)

9. I know you probably don't talk to absolute strangers, but I would like to meet you. (An approach of this type helps to calm down the con-

cerns many people—particularly women—have about talking to strangers.)

10. Please give me a couple of minutes to introduce myself. I'd like to meet you. (Although this one is tinged with a lack of self-confidence, it does convey a feeling of sincerity and honest intention.)

11. How did you manage to find a dress the exact same color as your eyes? (An advantage of this opener is that it conveys an interest in something about another person.)

12. Where are you flying to? (Used with most effectiveness at airports, this line is hackneyed but appropriate. Most people don't really fly that often and the question may be relatively new to them.)

13. Wow, look at the holding pattern (quarterback sneak, blitz, pirouette, swandive, finesse, backswing, etc.) (As mentioned earlier, a relevant and appropriate observation about the situation you and your prospect are placed in makes for a good opener.)

14. The pilot (tour leader, guide, etc.) looks pretty capable. (Another variation of the principle illustrated in opener 13.)

15. I'll bet your coat was designed in Paris. (Almost everybody enjoys hearing a compliment from a stranger.)

16. You have the most interesting walk. You stalk around like a panther. (Many women will enjoy hearing this since so few men comment upon a woman's walk except to note that her hips swing in a delightful manner.)

17. Who are you? (I personally endorse this line as being potent, but a few people will feel ill-at-ease because they are stuck for an answer. Loads of people have never stopped to ask themselves who they are.)

18. Hi, I wish I had a fabulous opening line. (Try this one. It works much better than you think. It is better suited for organized meeting places such as bars and resorts than spontaneous places such as parties, churches, and subways.)

19. I think I would like to get to know you. (Very safe, low key line that follows the "fumble a little principle." It can be used in almost all situations.)

20. It seems less crowded over here. (This is a non-threatening, non-pushy conversation opener. Your prospect is free to say nothing or talk.)

21. You look happy. (One reason this line is effective is that it leads to a discussion of how he or she really feels. Besides, it is a compliment to tell somebody they look happy.)

22. You look really involved in what's happening here. (Similar in impact to opener 21, but it has a stronger intellectual appeal.)

23. You look compassionate. (Prospective pick-ups will usually interpret this as a compliment. Of course a few may retort, "So what?")

24. I wish we had a mutual friend to introduce us. (A conversation opener of this type implies you are a modest person who feels self-conscious about pick-ups. This low key approach follows the "fumble a little principle.")

25. What do you think of that speaker (painting, call by the referee, third horse, etc.)? (Remember, appeals to another person's intellect can be quite effective as conversation openers.)

26. What do you think is wrong with the drummer? (People like to share with others what they think is inside information—that the drummer is hopped up on drugs. Whether this stereotype is true or false is unimportant. What counts is that it is a conversation opener.)

27. You are absolutely stunning. (Reserve this one for people who are genuinely attractive. Used indiscriminately, it may be taken as sarcasm.)

28. I bet men (or women) are forever trying to pick you up. (An indirect compliment of this type can be a good conversation opener. Usually your prospect will reply something like, "Why do you say that?" What better opening do you need?)

29. I bet you are here as an observer. (Underneath, many people feel self-conscious or defensive about having to resort to organized meeting places. Asking such a person this question implies that you think they are there by choice, not necessity.)

30. What do you do? (An element of bluntness is contained in this opener. Trouble comes only when the person feels compelled to hide or disguise his or her occupation. For instance, a typical response in a singles bar is, "I'm a secretary, but I really hate my job.")

31. Could you help me with a problem? I want to meet you, but I'm awkward at introducing myself to strangers. (Immediately, this puts you and your prospect in a complicated conversation. Used with sincerity, this can be highly effective. Girls who only want super-cool men will be repelled by this approach. Try it on conservative-looking men or women.)

35. You are somebody I would like to meet. (Openness and sincerity come across well with this approach. You are honestly and objectively stating the truth. An excellent way to start a relationship.)

33. What are you getting out of this course (lecture, movie, play, etc.)? (Another relevant appeal to another person's intellect. I highly recommend this conversation opener.)

34. What kind of luck have you had with this library? (You may find this even more effective in college than in public libraries. Nevertheless, use it if stuck for an opener in any library. If your prospect is having poor luck finding what he or she wants, you may have hit upon an ideal way to meet another person. Help out with a problem.)

35. It looks like you are involved in something important. (Implied here is a major compliment: Your prospect looks intelligent and serious enough to be committed to something other than themselves or picking up strangers. You might want to try this *avant-garde* opener soon.

36. I noticed you skiing down the hill (hitting the ball, coming off the green, doing a figure 8, etc.). It looks as if you've had lessons. (Again, you are making an appeal to something besides a person's physical appearance. You are communicating respect or admiration for something they have worked hard to develop. Very good.)

37. Did I see you on television talking about women's liberation (bussing, reform of abortion laws, pollution control, etc.)? (Use this approach only if you can do it with sincerity. However, if you get over this hurdle, it is potent. You are both flattering the person and giving them an opportunity to talk about an emotional topic.)

38. What would be a good way of meeting you? (Few people can refuse to respond to this question. Remember your goal is to get the person talking. What they say is much less important.)

39. You look like you know more about boating (skiing, scuba diving, macrame, fly casting, omelette making, etc.) than I do. (Another highly specific appeal to a person's skill or intellect. It works.)

40. I bet you know a great deal about

_____. (Plug anything in here, depending upon the situation. It is a simple, sincere statement. Even if the person is not knowledgeable about that topic, he or she will probably enjoy hearing the compliment.)

41. Hi, I would like to get your opinion on something. (A poet I know uses this with superb results in airports. He has two different closing lines to a poem. While waiting for a plane, or seated next to a female passenger, he asks for help in choosing the better closing line. He uses a closing line to a poem as an *opening* line for a relationship.)

42. I'd like to talk to you. (The honesty and sincerity of this opener has a positive effect on many people.)

43. I know that jokester who has been pestering you. He is much less sick than he appears. (Notice the subtle aspects to this opener. You are showing concern for a problem a girl might be having and you are also showing compassion for a fellow man. Women see these as admirable qualities in a man.)

44. What material is your dress (suit, coat, sweater, hat, etc.) made out of? (A side advantage here is that it provides a logical opportunity to touch your prospect.)

45. You have a perceptive look about you. (Another sophisticated compliment. Assuming that the other person understands the word "perceptive", you may provoke a good conversation.)

46. Hello. I've seen you at _____. We must have something in common. (A devastatingly effective line, providing you have actually seen the prospect before other than in an organized meeting place. You want something more in common to talk about than loneliness or an interest in bars.)

47. I bet you have a beautiful young girlfriend. (Any man will be flattered by this opener. It is almost as if you put an electronic probe into the pleasure center of his brain. Should the man not react to this statement, you can assume he is simply not interested in meeting you. Or perhaps he *does* have a beautiful young girlfriend.)

48. Look, I'm shy and I would like to meet you. (Many women like to help bring people out of their shyness. By simply talking to you, she might feel that she is doing something constructive— helping a shy person.)

49. Excuse me, but I can't help but admire a modern gal who doesn't dress like a sixteen-year-old. (Here is a powerful opener to use on a woman in her late thirties or early forties. It communicates the message that she is up-to-date and chic, but that she also has good sense. Also, and perhaps even more important, you are conveying acceptance of her age and her willingness to dress appropriately for her age.)

50. Say nothing. Just wink pleasantly at a man. (You don't have to be a research psychologist or a sexologist to know that nowhere in recorded history has a male ever rejected a wink from a woman he thinks is attractive.)

51. You look alone. Won't you join us? (This opener is best used by a man or woman with a group of like sexed friends who sees someone he or she would like to meet. Such an opener provides a valid reason for one man or woman to sit down with a whole group of people of the opposite sex. Introductions are inevitable in this kind of setting.)

52. You have interesting hands. (Commenting upon certain aspects of a stranger's body is good for opening conversation. Hands represent something

relatively neutral. Comments about sex organs, buttocks, breasts, thighs, or ears will probably result in rejection.)

53. What is your role here? (This question works well at conventions of psychologists, sociologists, psychiatrists, school teachers, or counselors. It can be taken seriously or as a joke. Either way it opens up an interesting line of dialogue.)

54. I wish more people were both intelligent and sexy. (Almost everybody enjoys a well-intended, well-reasoned compliment.)

55. Are you here collecting ideas for a book? (Particularly effective in an organized meeting place. It conveys the impression that you think the person doesn't need to be there and that they look intelligent.)

56. Hello, I'm doing some research about single people. May I ask you a few questions? (Students of mine will attest to the drawing power of this opener. Several dramatically improved their social life as a byproduct of working on this project!)

So far we have taken the positive approach. Fifty-six conversation openers have been suggested that may lead to sex, love, companionship and fun. Next, we will take the negative approach and look at some opening lines that could prevent a relationship from ever beginning. If you have ever been to the beach, a singles bar, a dance, or a party, you are probably familiar with the worst of these.

1. Haven't I met you some place before? (How un-cool, un-smooth, unimaginative, uninspired, and insipid do you want to appear?)

2. You are a beautiful person. (Ridiculous. Even if this cliché were true about that person, you need more than a first glance to determine if he or she is a "beautiful person.")

3. What are you drinking? (Uninspired and hackneyed.. However, effective if she has ordered an unusual drink.)

4. Let's fuck. (Used with some success by wise guys at parties and singles bars in New York and Los Angeles. However, you will turn off virtually every female with this crudity.)

5. How about some sexual intercourse? (A shade less crude than number four, but still an offensive, opening thrust.)

6. I love you. (Some people carry this off and start the prospect laughing. Most prospects, however, are simply turned off by such a frivolous opener.)

7. Do you think it will rain? (Old cornball lines should be avoided unless you are trying to engage old cornball-type people in conversation.)

8. Say, how about a date with me New Year's Eve? (I've seen this work once, simply because the girl burst into laughter. It's tantamount to saying, "I'm crazy or immature, take your pick.")

9. Are you Jewish (Italian, Polish, etc.)? (Never make an ethnic appeal. Most people interpret a statement from a stranger about their ethnic background as offensive. One good exception to the rule: It is okay to ask a person if he or she is Swedish. Nobody minds looking Swedish—unless, or course, they are Danish!).

10. You look like a movie star. (A wretched, old-fashioned line. The term "movie-star" is slowly losing its connotation of beauty. Why appear as if you learned your opening lines in the 1940's and 1950's?)

11. Would you like to dance with me the next time they play a slow number? (Wait until they play a slow number to ask her to dance. Use one of the other openers in the interim. Using this line

begins a relationship by your commenting that you lack a particular skill—dancing other than slow numbers.)

12. What church do you belong to? (A terrible social *faux pas*. Forget it.)

13. Are you alone? (Should your prospect be alone, he or she will feel uncomfortable. Girls suspect you are looking for a girl alone in order to bring her to your place. Or, they have to say, "Yes, I don't have a companion with me this evening." Men will take less offense to this question.)

14. You look lonely. (Bad, unless the prospect is really a needy, lonely individual who is seeking sympathy and support. People who have spent considerable time in sensitivity training or psychotherapy may not object to this opener.)

15. Do you believe in love at first sight? (Almost as bad as, "I love you.")

16. How many children do you have? (Bad because it has the connotation that the person is obviously divorced or separated; or that he or she is married but prospecting for an affair. Reserve this question for later in your initial conversation. Note that this line is well suited to a Parents Without Partners meeting.)

17. Why are you here? (A good way to put down somebody in an organized singles meeting place. It is almost as if you are provoking the person to say, ". . . because I'm lonely, bored, or desperate.")

18. Where have I seen you before? (I have saved the worst for last. You must be able to say something better than the most oft-repeated cliché in the singles game.)

Chapter 4

THE BEAUTIFUL BYPRODUCT

Under the best of circumstances, finding sex, love, companionship and fun is a byproduct of your being an interested and interesting person. People wrapped up in work, hobbies, or other people attract new relationships naturally. This chapter tells you how to capitalize upon this ideal method of meeting people and also how to avoid certain key mistakes. You will develop an understanding of how opposite-sexed people might mysteriously enter your life *without your making a deliberate effort to attract them.*

Celebrities Cannot Miss

Super-ideally, the way to meet opposite-sexed people is to become a celebrity. People in the public eye are sought after because of hero or heroine worship, *and* for other reasons. True or false, many people believe that a person who has caught the public attention is an interesting conversationalist and a worthwhile companion.

Celebrities are not sought after simply because they are wealthier and better looking than other people. Some celebrities don't conform to popular notions about physical attractiveness. Some celebrities earn moderate incomes: certain scientists, politicians and amateur athletes fit this category. The status and seeming importance celebrities have draw opposite-sexed people to them. Few readers of this book are celebrities or have the time, talent, or drive it takes to become one. But you can capitalize upon the same principle that gives celebrities such magnetic appeal. Whatever you can do to increase your worth as a person will give you some additional people-attracting-power. The celebrity principle is so important that it will be mentioned again in the next chapter. Next, let us look at the most basic way you can increase your worth as a person, thus increasing your appeal to other people.

Be Good at What You Do

One exciting way to attract the attention of other people is to be competent at your job or hobby. Competence is respected by almost everybody. People will want to meet you because you do something well, and you don't have to be a celebrity for this principle to work to your advantage. Bonnie, Darryl, and Janice are three good examples of this principle in action.

Bonnie was an excellent college student when she met her man, but it was not her ability as a student that led to him. During the summer, Bonnie took secretarial assignments for an office temporary firm. She was sent to Micro-Electronics to help them complete a lengthy customer report that was already behind schedule. Bonnie dug into the report as if she were the major stockholder at Micro-Electronics. She even typed away diligently one beautiful summer Sunday afternoon.

Larry, the engineer in charge of the project, was so concerned about meeting the deadline that he wouldn't have noticed if Bonnie were naked while typing the report. However, he did notice the superb typing job done on this complex, technical report. Larry asked Bonnie if he might take her to lunch as a token expression of his appreciation. Calmed down because the project deadline would be met, Larry noticed that Bonnie was a sharp and interesting person. She also noticed that, away from the pressures of a late report, he had some worthwhile qualities.

If Bonnie had taken the attitude that office temporary work was unimportant simply because it wasn't her life work—her major was anthropology—she might have done an ordinary job on her assignment at Micro-Electronics. An ordinary report would not have led to a luncheon date with Larry, the man she ultimately married.

Darryl is a competent tennis player. Twelve years of concentrated effort have given him a smooth-looking game, albeit below championship level. One summer Saturday, he was an invited guest at an exclusive racquet club in suburban Philadelphia. Despite the ninety degree heat, Darryl and his opponent—the number four man in the club—fought a blistering three set match. Edged out on the court, Darryl was triumphant off the court.

An intellectually alert, beautifully proportioned, dark-haired girl asked the club member, "Who is your friend with those thunderous backhands? I've never seen *him* at this club before." Darryl's friend replied, "You're right, he sure is tough, let me introduce you to him." The beautiful romance Darryl shared with Rosalind was well worth the twelve years he spent improving his game.

Janice designs and writes annual reports for clients of her public relations firm. Her biggest account led to her biggest romance. Janice had outdone herself in putting together an almost mod annual report for Company A. L.C., the President of Company A, was so pleased with the draft of this report that he asked the company controller to arrange a lunch between himself and that clever person who prepared the report. Janice called to confirm the luncheon date. L.C.'s secretary announced to him that his date with Miss Janice Wagner was confirmed. "Oh," said L.C., "I didn't realize the person working on our annual report is female. I am really looking forward to this luncheon."

No, Janice did not marry, live with, or even have an affair with L.C., the middle-aged president. Her exceptional skill in performing her job paid an even bigger dividend. During lunch, L.C. asked Janice if she had room for a new client. "Why, thank you very much," she replied, "I welcome challenging new assignments." L.C. then referred her to Jim, an adventuresome young man who founded his own company in the ecology field.

Jim's ecology company provided the proper environment for romance. Jim and Janice clicked, beginning it all with mutual respect for each other's expertise.

Keep on Sawing Wood

A slow but sometimes effective strategy for finding a mate or date is to proceed about your business as usual. In other words, just keep toiling in your vineyard, mending your carpets, or sawing your wood. Serendipity—that beautiful gift of finding valuable things not actively sought after —may come to your rescue. Remember, this book stresses not letting fate, luck, or serendipity *control* your social life: but happy, unplanned for events *can* happen to anybody.

Walter, a mining engineer from Ontario, worked for a Toronto construction engineering firm. Having recently split with his fiancée, Walter said to himself, "The blooming hell with it all. I'll just go about my business and forget about the lassies for awhile." Feeling this way, he eagerly took on an assignment to help repair some malfunctioning mining equipment on a remote site in Quebec. Serendipity reared its beautiful head. While on site, a lovely French Canadian journalist from Montreal interviewed Walter for a story about life in isolated mining towns. Walter is now a regular passenger on the Toronto-Montreal commuter flight. Georgette, the journalist he met on site, provides the meals and lodging.

Candy was depressed, discouraged, and unattached. She recently separated from her husband because, "From the first day of our honeymoon, all Bill wanted in a wife was a short order cook, sex partner, car washer, and errand runner." Instead of looking for a better replacement, Candy decided to improve her mind. "I have no interest in looking for men now." Candy happened upon a new romance by enrolling in a speed reading course. It all began when the instructor asked her out for coffee after class. Tim increased Candy's reading speed two hundred percent and her social life one hundred percent. Equally fortunate, Candy increased her comprehension of both what she reads and of the meaning of a good relationship with a man.

Have A Tight Schedule

Busy people—those who have a limited amount of time to invest in social life—often have the most exciting romances. An involved, occupied, tightly scheduled person projects an image of glamor and importance under most circumstances. If your tight schedule stems from something other than social life, this principle works the best. A good way to turn off a man is to say, "I'd love to go out with you but I have a date for the next ten consecutive nights." Similarly, one way to turn off a woman is to say, "I would like to work you into my schedule but I have six girls on my list right now. Perhaps I'll have a little more leeway in the spring."

People with loose schedules—those who can devote almost every night and weekend to social life —project an unimportant image. "Doesn't he (or she) do anything with his (her) time besides chase women (men)?" is the question people ask about the constant companionship seeker.

Brent's situation illustrates how having a loose schedule can hamper your chances of finding female companionship. A divorced father of three children, Brent sold office equipment. Brent was intent upon making up for the social life he had missed during fourteen years of marriage. He spent only a few hours per week with his children and cut his working day to a four P.M. finishing time. Brent made it clear to female prospects that he was a generous person who enjoyed spending money on women. Any preference they had for an expensive restaurant, he would happily oblige. He made frequent afternoon stops to the golf club in order to meet woman players. As his prospects became fewer, Brent asked one woman what he was doing wrong.

"Quite frankly, Brent, you are not painting a very good picture of yourself. You are supposed to be a father. I don't see any pictures of your children in your apartment. You never talk about them. When do you ever see them? It gives me a creepy feeling about you. And your job? I know many salesmen, and most of them work hard. I'm beginning to wonder if the only thing you really care about in life is dating women."

Paulette attracts the type of men she wants to attract in part due to her tight schedule (undeniably Paulette is also an intelligent, appealing person). The origins of her relationship with Cliff help explain how Paulette's schedule adds to her allure. Cliff, who she met in a music store, telephoned at 11:30 one Sunday morning.

"Hello, Paulette, this is Cliff Rawlings. We met at the Music Lover's Shop a couple of weeks ago. Remember, I asked you some questions about the difference between an expensive and a cheap guitar? Well I've called you about ten times. You never seem to be home. Are you tied up with one man?"

"No, I'm not emotionally involved with anybody right now. But I've been working overtime and I'm in a theatre group. We have rehearsals about four nights a week."

"Paulette, that sounds very interesting. Could we get together for a drink Wednesday night?" Paulette replied, "O.K. if you don't mind meeting me at around 10:30 after rehearsal. I think it would be fun to unwind." "Terrific," responded Cliff, "Where do I meet you?"

Ben presents another example of how a tight schedule can work in your favor. According to Ben, who travels constantly in his work, the only time he is successful in picking up women is when he is pressed for time. "Somehow, when I'm waiting around in an airport with lots of time to spare, no woman wants to talk to me. When I've got about ten minutes to check in before flight time, that's when a cute chick on line will signal me with her eyes. The same thing happens on the plane. When I open my attaché case to take out some important looking work, I'm much more likely to attract a woman than when I'm reading *Playboy* or *Field and Stream*.

"My best romance started when I was at O'Hare.

I was waiting for a plane to land that was to fly me to Los Angeles. A sharp girl was waiting for a later plane. I chatted with her briefly and learned that she worked in downtown Chicago. I told her I would be out-of-town for a week and handed her my business card. I asked her to jot down her name, phone, and address and to mail it to me. She did. Her note began, Dear Mr. Busy Executive.

"I called her and immediately I knew I did the right thing. If I had told a girl of her calibre that I would reschedule my flight in order to have a drink with her, she would have thought I was a Don Juan or a loafer."

The Rich Get Richer

Earning that first million dollars is the toughest; winning that first tournament is the biggest hurdle. Finding that first good relationship when you are unattached is also the most difficult. When you need a new relationship the least, that is precisely the time when you have the best chance of finding one.

Why is this cruel paradox true? One reason is that many people enjoy the challenge of trying to wrest away an attached person from his or her present lover. (Hopefully, the number of these types of people is diminishing, but you must be alert to their existence.) A more important reason is that being unattached, at least for too long, places you in an unfavorable light. Prospective opposite-sexed companions quietly ask themselves, "How come he (or she) has been on the loose so long? Is there something wrong that I'm not aware of? Afraid of lasting relationships? Flighty?"

How can "the rich get richer" principle work in your favor? By successively *trading-up* until the type of enduring relationship you want comes along. The same principle works in real estate. One way to own a $100,000 home is to start small and successively trade-up. Is this some kind of manipulative plot to buy and sell relationships until you find the one you want? Read further, it is much less callous than it sounds.

Mary, currently involved in a marriage she hopes lasts indefinitely, traded up to her husband in three steps. First, as she rejoined the singles scene after terminating a three year marriage, Mary broadened her definition of a suitable date.

"Al, an older fellow asked me out and I thought, 'Why not?' He didn't ask me out for the rest of my life, nor did I say the relationship would be permanent. He took me to some interesting restaurants and nice parties. I enjoyed his company, he enjoyed mine. I wasn't interested in having an affair, and he was happy just to share my companionship. The warmest thing I told him was that I appreciated the nice places he took me.

"At a Christmas dance given by his company, I met Chuck, a man much younger than Al. Chuck was all man but not husband material. He was a sexual athlete and loads of fun. His main ambition in life was to have sexual relations with 500 women. According to his collection of old calendars, I was his 215th, and his experience certainly showed.

"Chuck was great and I saw him regularly until I met Burt, my husband. Burt was an admirer and friend of Chuck's. He figured that any girl sharp enough to date Chuck must have something on the ball. Chuck was quite willing for me to date Burt, because he knew that I wanted to find a husband and he cared about my welfare.

"You could say that, for me, Al was good, Chuck was better, and Burt was best. I don't think anybody got hurt in that deal."

Earlier in this book I recommended that you define attractiveness in your own terms. An attractive person is somebody *you* think has many positive qualities. However, the "rich get richer" principle will not work for you unless your tastes are similar to many others. Once prospective dates and mates are convinced that you are appealing to attractive people of the opposite sex, they will feel complimented when you turn on to them.

People new in your life enjoy bragging about the calibre of your former lovers. Not uncommon are statements such as these: "Dan was married to a really attractive gal," "Eva has gone out with some pretty important men," "Did you know that my Chet actually had an affair with a model in New York before we started dating?" "I was lucky to find Joan. So many men would have wanted her for themselves."

Help A Friend Find Romance

Matchmakers often make out quite well themselves in the romance department. Helping somebody else find a decent social life may produce a beautiful byproduct for you. As you proceed to fix somebody else up, you may get fixed up yourself. The act of trying to help another lonely human being puts you in a favorable light. "My what a compassionate and giving person Lola is. She takes time from her own busy schedule to help a friend."

Helping a friend find romance has a psychological effect on people that can work to your advantage. When you approach another individual and mention that you want to introduce him (or her) to a friend you are paying that person a powerful compliment. You are saying by your actions, "I think highly enough of you to recommend you to a friend." A few skeptics with poor self-images will say, "Why the hell does he think I need to be fixed up," but most people will be flattered.

How can flattering another person improve your social life? Everytime you create a new friend or solidify relationships with an old one, you have increased your chance of meeting another opposite-sexed person for yourself. For instance, in appreciation that person might invite you to a party where your prince or princess charming could be waiting.

Bruce, a very low-ranking faculty member at a big university helped himself by helping a higher faculty member find romance. Kurt, an associate professor asked Bruce an assistant instructor (only under-ranked by the students themselves) the age old question, "How do you meet a woman?" Energetic Bruce replied, "Kurt this is a big weekend on campus. I have just the plan for you. Come along with me to a dance sponsored by one of the girls dormitories (this was in the era of sex-segregated college living). It should be good. A lot of coeds attend these things and many of them probably would like to meet an older guy. Besides, being a faculty member will give you an edge over the undergraduate fellows. I'll show you how it's done."

Kurt found the evening a good investment. He met Ursula, a graduate student in chemistry, and dated her for two months. Bruce, however, came away with first prize. After the last dance number was played, Bruce spotted a pretty young woman. Leaning against a post, with a glass of fruit punch clenched in his hand, he calmly said, "Hello, my name is Bruce. What's yours?"

Twenty minutes later, Bruce and that alert

young sophomore from Chicago shared a cup of coffee. Within twelve months they shared the same last name. Bruce has never forgotten that evening at the dormitory dance.

Linda is another person who reaped personal gain from helping somebody else find romance. Carole, who Linda met at a modern dance class, asked her a personal favor. "Do you know anybody you can introduce me to? I'm not going with anybody now and I'm not getting any younger." Linda was sympathetic, but she did not take immediate action. The following week, Carole pressed further. "Did you find anybody for me yet?"

Linda decided that Carole must be desperate so she proceeded to take action. Five names of remote possibilities occurred to Linda, and she called them all. Two said they refuse to go on blind dates; one said he was now living with a girl; one said, "O.K., give me Carole's phone number and I'll call her. She sounds like the type of person I want to meet."

Barney, the fifth man contacted by Linda had a different response. "Linda, I would much rather go out with a charming girl like you than get fixed up with somebody I don't even know. Let's you and I get together." Barney and Linda did get together and dated for several months.

What Do You Enjoy Besides Sex?

Another way of stating the beautiful byproduct principle is that your chance of meeting someone are the best when you are an interesting, well integrated person. People who attract other people generally are not those people who put the most energy into attracting people. Attractiveness to other people is a byproduct of having well developed interests *other than in meeting people*. Even more damaging to potential relationships is to be interested only in sex. Gordie and Alma are preoccupied with sex and it works to both their disadvantages.

Gordie frequents singles bars to keep himself supplied with leads for his social life. Despite his good looks and charm, Gordie aborts more relationships than he would like. Priscilla, an observant girl who dated Gordie twice, explains what he does wrong.

"Gordie, I'm afraid to say, is a real character, if not a sex maniac. He stands there in the bar with all his finery; a pinkie ring, the latest style suit and handcrafted Italian shoes. A girl can't talk to Gordie more than five minutes before he brings up the topic of sex. The first comment he made to me was, 'My that's a virginal looking dress. I hope it isn't significant.' Then he starts talking about how wonderful it is that we no longer live in the Victorian age and people can express themselves freely. I thought he was kind of kooky, but I did go out with him when he called.

"Gordie took me to an Armenian restaurant on our first date. He went into a lecture about how Armenian food contains aphrodisiacs such as bay leaves and exotic herbs. He then ordered a Portuguese Chablis wine that he claimed also stimulated sexual desire. I tried to change the subject to movies. Gordie went on at length about how important it was that a person no longer need to study medical texts in order to see human genitalia displayed in clinical detail. People could now see it all at their local movie house.

"To get Gordie off his sex talk, I asked him about his family. He claimed that he really disliked his family and had nothing to do with them. He gave me a little dig by noting that a romantic restaurant was no place to talk about something as unsophisticated as family life.

"Next, I asked Gordie about his job. I figured that might be a good topic because he dressed like an executive in an advertising agency. Gordie parried that one, too. He told me that he was working well below his capability but it did not bother him. He claimed to be a true epicure whose life was more oriented toward romance than work.

"Asking Gordie about hobbies or sports was equally fruitless. I got the impression that the closest thing to athletics in his life was sunbathing by the pool. His comment about sports was, 'I am indeed a true believer in what Freud had to say. Men who participate in sports do so only because they are not getting all the sex their body craves.'

"Exasperated, all I could say was, 'Gordie, what do you enjoy besides sex?' "

Alma has no trouble finding men for brief affairs, but she does have trouble attracting lasting relationships with the sincere mature type of man she wants. When former boyfriends of Alma are asked, "What is she like," the response is usually, "loads of fun," "kicks," "fun-loving," or "see for yourself." Alma is never described: "There's a fascinating, interesting woman."

Alma, like Gordie, orients most of her life around sex. Unfortunately for Alma's sake, it works to her disadvantage. Her lack of interests outside of sex gives her a nymphomaniac tinge that aborts many relationships. Alma is so interested in sex, to the exclusion of anything else, that she seems shallow and unreal. What does she do that conveys this impression?

Alma's bedroom features a king-sized bed, studded with soft, luxurious pillows. When dates arrive she turns on the psychedelic lights and soft music. Her collection of lingerie is reminiscent of the working attire of an exotic dancer. During a movie, Alma virtually sits on her date's lap. Her usual response to an invitation out is something like, "Fine, so long as we get back early enough to spend lots of time alone together."

Conversing with Alma is amusing but frustrating. Her response to general conversation is, "But darling why talk about other things, when we can talk about romance?"

Is Marriage Your Only Interest?

Don't carry around a large placard saying, "I'm looking for a husband (or wife)" if you want the beautiful byproduct principle to work for you. Earlier in this book I mentioned that talking about marriage too soon in a relationship is a desperate tactic. In addition, a preoccupation with thoughts about marriage can decrease your chances of attracting somebody worthwhile. Only people themselves desperate want to date another person whose number one interest is marriage. A conversation with Faith illustrates the thinking of a girl more interested in marriage itself than in *any one particular man.*

"Faith what plans do you have for the new year?"

"I hope to get married by December."

"Anybody I know? Tell me about him."

"Oh, I'm not dating anybody special right now. It's just that I'm sick and tired of coming home to an empty apartment at night. This year I'm going to find a husband."

"What kind of a man do you want?"

"One who likes marriage and children. I can adjust to most other things."

Pat, a 51 year old widower, was successfully married for twenty-five years. Lonely, depressed, and discouraged, he actively sought a replacement for his wife. His intentions quickly became known in the small circles in which he traveled. Pat's friends saw him as a sad person who was urgently looking for a wife.

Pat was preventing the beautiful byproduct principle from working in his favor. Many women would be interested in meeting a man of Pat's calibre. A plant superintendent by occupation, Pat was also interested in boating and camping—activities he could share with a new family. However, Pat became known as a wife-hunting widower rather than primarily as an interesting and worthwhile person. Ellie, a woman who dated Pat, describes how he operates.

"Pat and I met on a blind date. A friend of mine told me about him and gave him my number. He called and invited me to dinner. Pat was a gentleman but I think he felt awkward going on a date. I don't think he and his wife went out much. For most of the evening, he talked about his wife and how she died. It was a pleasant evening, but certainly not a very happy one.

"Pat next took me for a ride in his cabin cruiser and he seemed a little more cheerful. He talked in such positive terms about his marriage and his children. Even his boat was named after his late wife. On the third date, Pat hit me with a bombshell. He said, 'Look Ellie, you seem like a very nice person. I'm a very busy man and I hate to waste time on dates. If you are not at all interested in marrying me, let's stop seeing each other right now. I'm not proposing, I just want to know if you could ever see yourself married to me.'

"It hurt our relationship and I could only say, 'Pat are you seriously interested in me as a person, or is marriage your only interest?' "

Chapter 5

IMPROMPTU SITUATIONS

Sex, love, companionship, and fun can be found economically and efficiently. Prospects can be located and picked up in the normal course of daily living. Special efforts such as joining clubs, taking courses, asking friends to fix you up, or taking a singles cruise are not the only way to meet people. Endless possibilities exist for picking up people in natural, unorganized situations. All that is required is that you raise your people-finding antenna and use an appropriate opening line when a prospect moves into range. Earlier in this book I discussed *how* to play the singles game; this is the first chapter on *where* to play.

Impromptu situations fall somewhat into the category of *good luck*. However, when you help luck along, you are moving into the territory emphasized in my next chapter, "Systematic Efforts." Don't become too concerned with semantics in your quest for companionship. The boundaries between impromptu situations and systematic efforts often blur.

Airports and Airplanes

Thousands of good relationships have begun in airports and airplanes, and not only between stewardesses and passengers. Commenting about the weather may be trite outside the airport, but it makes a very relevant opening line in the context of air travel. Everybody—including the most seasoned pilot—has some underlying anxiety about flying conditions. Commenting to that man or woman ahead of you in line, "It looks like very comfortable weather for flying," is a reassuring note that gets most people talking.

Boarding the plane last, contrary to popular opinion, is not the best approach to finding somebody interesting to sit next to. Board early, fumble around at the coat or magazine rack until you have spotted a prospect, then position yourself. If you board last you will lose out in the competition that takes place for sitting next to an attractive person.

Amusement Parks

Amusement parks are on the decline in popularity, but they are still a haven for divorced and separated fathers exercising their Sunday visitation rights. For openers, how about: "Could your boy and my girl share the same boat? I notice they are about the same size." Matching up the children can be an effective start to matching up the parents!

Apartment Building

Possibilities for meeting people abound for apartment dwellers. Be mindful of a wide variety of impromptu contacts. Males and females both have to dump garbage in the incinerator, wash clothing in the laundry room, shovel their car out of snow, or scrape their windshields on cold, icy mornings. If you haven't already investigated the pool side people meeting possibilities, read this book again from the beginning. Conversing with other-sexed people in the elevator is another daily opportunity of merit. Should you lock yourself out of your apartment, ask an attractive-looking prospect if you can use his or her phone.

Creativity may sometimes be required to capitalize upon the source of unattached woman and manpower in apartment buildings. The next time you need to borrow a corkscrew (seasoning, hammer, phillip's head screwdriver, etc.) knock on the door of a neighbor you would like to meet. Why not ask that interesting prospect down the hall to take care of your plants while you are on your week vacation or business trip?

Vary your daily habits. Take your wash to different laundry rooms; dump your garbage in different incinerators. (You can always say the incinerator was blocked on your floor or that the laundry closest to you was busy.) Swim in the pool at different hours, leave for work at different times in the morning. Pleasant surprises are more likely to happen when you increase your range of potential chance encounters.

Apartment Hunting

When hunting for a new apartment for yourself, take careful note of other people visiting the same building for similar purposes. Discussing the difficulties in finding a suitable apartment is a natural common base for conversation. Combine apartment and people hunting; it's more fun and profitable than apartment hunting alone.

Attorney

Next time you visit your attorney on business, casually ask him if any of his clients might be interested in meeting you. Attorneys spend much of their professional time processing divorces and they become quite knowledgeable about the character and financial status of their clients. The happiest couple I know met through a mutual attorney. Incidentally, while waiting for your lawyer, don't neglect to see what prospects might be sitting right there in his waiting room.

Automobile Accident

Non-serious automobile accidents can lead to serious relationships. Next time you are involved in a fender bumping incident be careful to get the names and phone numbers of interesting looking victims and witnesses. Cliff plowed into the rear end of another car at a stop light. He was courteous and apologetic to both the driver and passenger in the injured car. Sensing some romantic possibilities, Cliff insisted on getting the female passenger's name and phone number just in case whiplash injuries later developed.

Impressed by his concern, she was willing to date him when he called several days later. Cliff, our careless driver, suffered a slight increase in his insurance premiums but the romance that developed out of the situation was worth it.

Avon Lady

Why overlook an obvious possibility? The Avon lady might have more to offer than a variety of toiletries and cosmetics. Even the stingiest of men will admit that it is worth the investment of one bottle of cologne to determine if you and the Avon lady can get something going. Remember, she has to come back to deliver your order which gives you a second chance to become acquainted.

Cafeterias

Cafeterias create more favorable situations for meeting people than do restaurants. Company, school, or hospital cafeterias are better than public ones. Cafeteria etiquette allows you to sit adjacent to anybody providing there is an empty chair at his or her table. "Hi, my name is——" is an opener that fits naturally into the cafeteria scene. Why not get more for your money than a mediocre meal the next time you use a cafeteria?

Celebrity

Here is the best documented, most accurate statement in this book: Big-time male celebrities are amply supplied with women. Can you imagine the quarterback for the New York Jets, a best-selling male novelist, or a Nobel Prize-winning scientist having to resort to computer dating? Women find accomplishment sexy and even minor celebrities find plenty of situations in which females take the initiative to meet them. In short, if you want to meet women in the most effortless, natural way, devote your life to becoming well-known for something.

Women celebrities also do quite well in the people-meeting department, but not quite as well as male celebrities. Why? In spite of the advances made by feminism, many males are still threatened by female accomplishment. As told to me by an accomplished woman in the arts, "If I were male, I would have all kinds of women chasing me. I'm said to be attractive and brilliant. I'm female, so very few males know how to relate to me."

Damsel in Distress

Ancient in origin, this impromptu situation is still one of the most effective methods of meeting people. Provide assistance to a stranger and the first step in a relationship has begun. Here is my favorite application of this idea. John noticed a woman having difficulty cashing a check for groceries in a supermarket. Apparently, she lacked appropriate identification. Swiftly, he moved in and volunteered to cash a check for this damsel in distress. As things worked out, John had a splendid affair for cashing an $8.72 check that did not even bounce. Helping a woman fix a flat, adjust a ski binding, or pick up a bag of spilled groceries are all variations on the same theme.

Providing on-the-spot assistance to men in distress is correspondingly a potent way for women to get things started with men. One approach is to help a man *prevent* distress. Should you spot a man in a laundromat about to wash blue jeans and white tee shirts together, you can rescue him from a problem about to beset him.

Road maps provide a good opportunity to work the person-in-distress routine. Whenever you spot somebody fidgeting with a road map, move in to help uncomplicate matters. Even if you just provide reassurance that the stranger has chosen the best route, you have started a conversation by taking a sincere interest in that person's problem.

Demonstrations

Should you participate in a public demonstration, check out the social possibilities. Logic and rumor indicate that people who participate in public demonstrations are liberated both politically and sexually. Past newspaper accounts of some of the large scale peace demonstrations tell of couples who have publically engaged in intercourse. Should your preferences be more conservative, simply try for a conversation with a demonstrator. Try this opener if nothing else comes to mind, "Let's say you and I get together after the revolution."

Dog Walking

Walking your dog comes up so often in discussions about meeting people that it might also be considered an organized strategy. Dogs help people get into some conversation starting, spontaneous situations. Women are often more receptive to an approach that mentions their dog than one that directly mentions them. Thus, "You must spend hours grooming your schnauzer," is more socially acceptable than, "You must spend hours grooming your hair."

Dog fanciers are sometimes embarrassed when their pet urinates against somebody else's property. Potent, people-meeting opportunities can be made of such situations. For example, a girl with a great dane might say to a prospect, "Pardon me, sir, my dog just splashed your hubcap. Is there anything I can do to repair the damage?"

Fate

Many people still believe that finding the right person for yourself is strictly a matter of fate or chance, thus they put no effort into finding sex, love, companionship and fun. Fate sometimes does work, but it is a very slow process. One woman met her lover because he and she shared an elevator during a power failure. An attorney in New York City met his mate because she occupied the bed next to him when he donated blood.

Even if you believe that somehow God will furnish you with the mate of your dreams, you still have to help Him or Her along. Keep those people-finding antennae erect and take careful note when some divine force sends a good prospect in your direction.

Greeting Cards

Greeting cards can be an effective way of catching someone else's attention. Christmas cards, because they are so indiscriminately used, are not nearly as effective as cards sent for other occasions. Suppose Alice has been trying to meet Ralph, a widowed excutive she has been too timid to directly call and ask for a date. Should Alice note in the newspaper that Ralph has been promoted (or elected to the School Board or anything else), she might send him a card of congratulations. Sympathy cards, if done with considerable sensitivity, can also trigger a relationship.

With a little ingenuity, you can find a legitimate reason to send almost anybody a card at almost anytime of the year. What about a Mother's Day card to that cute divorcée you have noticed but haven't yet met. Inscribe with something like this: "I know you are not my mother, but who says Mother's Day cards are only from your own children?" Follow up the card with a call. When holidays or special occasions are not in the offing, a simple "note from a friend" card will suffice.

An enterprising secretary in Detroit sent a male social worker a card saying, "I admire the way you help people. Keep up the good work." An exclusive relationship with the social worker did not develop, but at least they shared a pleasant short term relationship.

Date's Friend

Never overlook the possibility of recruiting new prospects among the friends and acquaintances of a date. When your date says, "I have to drop something off at my girlfriend's house," volunteer to take her. Your date's girlfriend and you might possibly turn on to each other. Suppose you are lukewarm toward a tennis player you are dating. When he suggests that you come along to watch him play tennis, cooperate. His tennis partner could become your life partner.

Calling your date's friend presents some difficulty, but here is a workable strategy. Praise your mutual friend, but explain that (as your mutual friend may have already told you) yours is only a casual relationship. Suggest that you would like the opportunity to get to know her, but only if your mutual friend would not be highly offended. The openness and compassion suggested by this approach is a proven winner.

While we are on the subject of bird-dogging, don't neglect the possibilities of the dates of your own friends. Make sure first that your friend is not seriously involved (or hopes to become involved) with that particular date.

Funerals

Funerals, similar to any other gatherings of people, are plausible (I did not say exceptional) places to meet new people. I strongly recommend against extending an on-the-spot social invitation to the buried person's close friend, relative, or spouse. Later that week, sending a message of concern to the bereaved can be a good relationship starter. Be alert to prospects at the funeral who are not that closely associated with the person buried. You and that person have a natural shared experience; both of you feel sorrow for the dead person or you would not be there.

Highways

Cruising along the highway at sixty-five miles an hour is not the time for prospecting, but you have to slow down sometime. Debbie, a physically and psychologically attractive person, reports how she started a nice romance on the highways. "I was driving on the outskirts of town, when I saw a blond haired, blue eyed state trooper. He was straight out of Hollywood. Naturally, I smiled.

He turned on his big red light and had me pull over. In a very proper way he asked for my identification, and said that everything was okay. When he was off-duty he called me and asked for a date."

Another approach is to carefully look around when you pull into a service plaza adjacent to a throughway. Vacationers are often willing to talk to strangers. Chatting with people in a hippie-type van is a natural. Ski racks on the top of cars give you another plausible reason for opening a conversation.

Humorous, Awkward Incidents

Asked how she met her drummer husband, Sharon replied: "One night about two years ago I was with a date at my favorite night club. The floor wasn't crowded so I tried a few really way-out steps. Bang. I fell on the floor and was my face red. My date was stunned, but the drummer put down his sticks and helped me up. As corny as it sounds, I said, 'I guess I have really fallen for your music.' We both laughed and he asked me for my name. He called me the next day."

Quick thinking people have capitalized upon spilling food or drinks on others in public places. Having food or drink spilt on your parka can be funny, but a martini-drenched braless gown is much less reason for instant friendship and conversation.

Job Situations

My next chapter, "Systematic Efforts," includes suggestions about choosing companies or careers that offer good people-finding opportunities. Of concern here are those multitude of day-by-day possibilities for finding your mate or date at work. Above all, you have to break out of your normal work routine and keep alert to prospects. When you are asked to serve on a company wide safety committee, say yes with *elan*. Your elan may lead to an Alan or an Elaine who is also on that safety committee. Don't wait for interoffice correspondence to take three days to deliver that important memo to a department on the third floor. Deliver it in person. Every time you walk into a new department you are increasing your chances for an impromptu meeting with a person of the opposite sex.

Brian, a young engineer, walked into a new department and spotted a girl who immediately turned him on by her appearance and mannerisms. He asked a work-related question that led to a marriage that is still going strong after five years: "Pardon me, do you handle the engineering inventory file?"

Hanging out by the water cooler is yesterday's cliche; an occasional trip to the Xerox machine is more modern and more effective. Large numbers of people visit the Xerox machine. Go there with a legitimate purpose; otherwise you will be perceived as odd, lonely, horny (or all three) by prospects. Caution: Sometimes people waiting in line to use the office copier can be quite impatient and unfriendly. You may have to overcome their moods.

Welcome the opportunity to attend company picnics, banquets, and recreational activities. Capitalize on the chance to meet new people in your organization. You always have one thing in common to engage your prospect in conversation—you both work for the same employer. While you are prospecting, remember one key guideline: Exercise extreme caution in becoming involved with somebody in your immediate work area. Will the pleasure of getting involved with that person be worth the embarrassment of running into him or her every other day should you two split? People who have tried it recognize the awkwardness of working professionally with a former lover.

Even the most mundane job can lead to a big romance, as illustrated by the case of a young Norwegian maid, Anne-Marie Rosmussen. Her ten year marriage to Stephen Rockefeller stemmed from her place of employment—his house.

Job Hunting

Keep alert to promising people-hunting opportunities while job hunting. Applying for a job provides a legitimate excuse to visit different organizations where many attractively dressed, employed, well adjusted people congregate. In many companies your job hunting effort will get you no further than the personnel office. Salvage the situation. Perhaps that warm and considerate personnel specialist is unattached. Remember, most personnel specialists are people minded and thus make interesting social companions. Be prepared to strike up a conversation with other people sitting in the company lobby. Isn't it much better to meet a salesman or a saleswoman in a job situation than at a bar? You will look much more important to a prospective lover if you are reading a company annual report than if you are ordering a scotch and soda.

Libraries

While developing yourself intellectually, you may be able to develop yourself socially. Many good romances begin in libraries. A standard opener is, "What kind of luck are you having finding what you want here?" Public libraries are better suited for prospecting nights and weekends than on weekdays. College libraries are good anytime. Should you need to gather information for a report, choose a college library over a public library; particularly if you like bright young girls (or boys).

Inevitably you will need some assistance in the library, even if it is just for operating the copying machine. Capitalize upon this situation by asking somebody that looks interesting to you for help.

Another reliable technique for picking up people in libraries is to make relevant comments about book jackets. Here is how it works. Suppose Ginny spots an interesting looking man studying a book about acupuncture. She comments, "Wow, I didn't realize that anybody had written a whole book about that fascinating technique." Unless that interesting-looking man is a social retard (or hopelessly in love with somebody else), a conversation between Ginny and a stranger will ensue. As I mentioned earlier, every relationship begins with a conversation.

Museums

Art museums have become a popular meeting ground for unattached people. I have included museums under "impromptu situations" because it is assumed that you have some interest in visiting museums other than prospecting for people. Serious, intellectual people, as one would expect, frequent museums. If your only interest in art is social, you will create a negative impression on the typical museum visitor.

Pick-up maneuvers in museums follow a pattern. Should your prospect be interested in becoming acquainted with you, he or she will respond to your first opener. In contrast, if your prospect gives you a "Drop dead brother" look with her eyes, move on to the next object d'art.

Use your imagination to go one step beyond the stereotyped opener, "What do you think of that painting?" Suppose you and a prospect are observing a painting by a French impressionist. Communicate a personal feeling, such as, "Somehow all those soft colors bring me down a bit." Sensitive people enjoy responding to feelings, even those of strangers.

Parks

Parks are losing ground as a good place to pick up strangers, particularly in major cities. Somehow a man has to communicate the message, "Don't worry, stranger, I am not a rapist or mugger, nor am I criminally insane." This is hard to do—especially if you happen to look the part! While strolling through the park, be alert to opportunities for helping people retrieve unleashed dogs, fight off park derelicts, or repair a flat bicycle tire.

Playgrounds

Playgrounds within public parks present a different challenge. They are well suited for beginning affairs with bored housewives, but are also a source of divorced people. Above all, a man should never enter a playground unescorted by children. Immediately people will say to themselves, "I wonder what that dirty old pervert is doing in this playground."

One good approach is to bring your children to the playground on a regular basis. A camaraderie develops naturally after you have been seen there several times. Aside from doing something nice for your children, you may wind up doing something very nice for yourself (such as starting a terrific romance, when your child extends a luncheon invitation to his or her new friend).

Professional Helpers

Everybody needs professional help. Who never, ever visits a dentist, doctor, lawyer, psychotherapist, marriage counselor or tax accountant? Keep those antennae up. Psychiatrists and psychologists sometimes do have affairs with their patients, however unethical this practice is looked upon by most of them. Members of the clergy don't deliver all their inspiring messages from the pulpit.

Professional helpers are often in the enviable position of having natural excuses for body contact with the people they are being paid to help. Barbara, a dental hygienist, notes that when she is not interested in turning on to a patient she cleans his teeth as if she were playing a concert piano. When Barbara *is* interested in turning on to a prospect she gently brushes her firm little breasts against him (all in the line of duty).

Gynecologists are much less likely to do their prospecting through the type of body contact they have with patients. One Harvard Medical School professor tells his male students in advance, "Remember, fellows, one finger socially, two fingers professionally." Physicians worry about a malpractice suit stemming from any misinterpretation of the way in which they conduct a physical examination. No man in history, however, has ever tried to sue a dental hygienist or nurse because she brushed against him or tenderly touched his body.

Restaurants

Restaurants are not organized meeting places for singles. Thus you can appear cool and sophisticated if you happen upon somebody promising while dining. The ancient technique of asking your waiter to deliver a message to a prospect seated across the restaurant still works.

Lunch counters are more effective than restaurants. Placed elbow to elbow with a stranger, you can readily begin some kind of conversation beyond, "Could you please pass me the ketchup." You might try this one: "How come everybody looks so lonely when they are eating at a lunch counter?"

Service Stations

Alex started a high-powered romance while filling up at the high-test pump. Your chances of being equally lucky are slim, but if it happened to somebody else it could happen to you. While waiting for gasoline, scan the station. Assume you like the rugged mechanic type. You might make one happy by asking him, "Aren't you worried about that car falling on top of you?" Mechanics usually aren't too smooth socially and may need to be helped along conversationally.

Service stations give you an opportunity to try a few sexually symbolic opening lines that electrify the car buff. How about, "Say, fellow, I bet you have a lot of power in that machine of yours."

Sports

Athletics of all types provide you natural opportunities to seize upon impromptu situations. People often take up sports such as skiing and tennis for the sole purpose of meeting other people. Prospects are much more impressed when you have an authentic interest in sports. Skill also helps. Real sports enthusiasts are more likely to find you interesting when you are competent in the sport that has brought you together.

Downplaying your skill to a prospect is cool; exaggerating your skill puts you in an unfavorable light. Imagine telling a girl in the ski lodge that you are an advanced skier (when you are an absolute novice) and finding out later that she races competitively!

Take advantage of the benefits of asking for or giving help. For instance, should you notice a girl bowler throwing too many gutter balls, you might comment: "I think I have a suggestion that might help keep your ball in the lane." Girls should not be hesitant to offer sports tips to men, particularly if they are looking for secure males. Suppose you note an attractive male skier who is taking his lumps on the slopes. Down at the chair lift, you might comment, "I noticed you were having some difficulty on those sharp turns. I know a technique that you might find helpful."

Stores

"The very best way to meet single men," says Jeanne, "is food shopping on Sunday afternoon or late at night. If you want to meet the playboy type, go to the department where they sell those fancy frozen hors d'oeuvres." Supermarkets can be super places for meeting people and so can most retail stores. You increase the odds of a favorable impromptu situation for yourself if you shop in places where the type of people you want to meet shop. While shopping for expensive ties for your present boyfriend, you may encounter a man who shares similar tastes. Conversely, if you buy your girlfriend discount nylon panties, the type of girls you meet will be those who wear discount nylon panties.

Delay your food shopping until past ten at night when all the family people have gone home.

Except for night shift production workers, policemen, and some maintenance workers, most midnight shoppers are single. Supermarkets at two A.M. have a cozy atmosphere amenable to polite conversation.

While shopping, be mindful of the prospects of picking up salesclerks. Don't ignore that middle-aged appliance salesman at Sears. Most of them have bigger retirement benefits than executives in industrial corporations. Quite often, writers, actors, and students take part-time sales jobs to help defray expenses.

Bob, a young man who keeps amply supplied with women, tells how he capitalized upon a situation to meet his present roommate:

"I was at a drugstore buying some envelopes. In walks a groovy chick who really catches my eye. Not knowing what to do next, I asked her if she knew where they keep the suntan lotion. Then I asked her advice about the best lotion. She told me and then I asked her questions about the best place for swimming. Next, I invited her swimming that afternoon. Two months later we were living together and I hope it lasts forever."

Streets

Picking up people in the streets and other public places has less of a social stigma today than in the past. Impromptu approaches, of course, are much preferable to stalking the streets looking for action. Occasionally, fabulous romances begin on city sidewalks. As told in *Cosmopolitan,* one fashionable divorcée met the Chairman of the Board of a large airline on a Manhattan street corner. Coming out of a Carnegie Hall concert, he smiled and asked her for a drink. Having a daughter waiting at home, she opted for his coming to her house. Their later adventures included weekend airplane flights to faraway resorts.

Albert Ellis, the prominent sexologist, strongly recommends that women take the initiative in picking up men on the streets. Dr. Ellis contends that your choice is almost unlimited. Should a woman wait for men to pick her up, she is limiting herself to a handful of undesirable men. After a few minutes of conversation with a stranger, you can determine whether or not to carry it one step further. Contrary to popular opinion, just because a woman takes the initiative in meeting a man she is not implying, "Let's hop into bed."

Students

Teachers meet a vast supply of potential dates or mates in their daily work. Conservative in nature, most college professors and high school teachers, feel some giant taboo exists about prospecting for companionship among former students. Jim, a male high school teacher, asked former students for dates whether or not they showed signs of being interested. After telephone calls to about twenty five different high school seniors, word got around and Jim was asked to resign. But done with sensitivity—not indiscriminately—students are fair game.

What about teachers as prospects? Your friendly old prof might want to date you, but he may need some encouragement from you before making the first move. Why not ask for an appointment to see him during office hours and then proceed to talk about general topics?

Female professors might also welcome the opportunity to become romantically involved with a student. Even if your favorite woman professor cannot accept your offer, it will flatter her ego to have been asked out by a student.

Caution. Wait until the course is over and you have already received your grade before asking out or accepting a date from a professor. Imagine how awkward it feels to complain to the dean of the college that you think you received a failing grade because you refused to sleep with your professor.

Trade and Service People

Romantic possibilities can present themselves anytime you have a one-to-one business relationship with somebody else. Earlier we talked about enlarging your social life through contacts with doctors, dentists, lawyers, and other professionals. Don't neglect the gamut of other service people in your life. Plumbers, carpenters, tow truck drivers, cab drivers, real estate salesmen, septic tank specialists, and even special tutors for your sick child represent real possibilities. Lady Chatterly knew all about the sexual prowess of gardeners!

Again, you have to make the first move. Your friendly taxicab driver may fear that you will complain to the company if he (or she) makes a pass at you.

Vacation Travel

Mike, a stock broker from Philadelphia, met Annette, a speech therapist from Baltimore, while they were bicycling in Bermuda. Mike and Annette clicked and the one hundred miles separating them back home has not prevented a beautiful romance from developing. Thousands of romances have similarly begun when two people met each other spontaneously on vacation. (Later, we'll have something to say about those organized vacations for singles.) *Spontaneous*, of course, does not mean that you are not obliged to take advantage of promising impromptu situations.

Your chances of making a big score on vacations are much better if you travel alone than if you stay in the constant companionship of friends. Experienced travellers will tell you that the best way to chase away men on your vacation is to travel with several other girls. A girl multiplies her chances of meeting men on vacation about fifty times when she travels alone. As explained by Ruth, an attractive administrative assistant:

"The absolute best way to meet a man is to travel Euro-Rail. Never in my life did I find so many men in a short period of time as I did on those fantastic European trains. You can't miss unless you wear a nun's outfit. I like businessmen so traveling first class made sense for me. If you like poor men or students, travel second class.

"Because you have unlimited travel, some girls would get off the train and spend a weekend with one guy. After that was over they would get back on the train and find somebody else. One girl I heard about ended up staying in a castle for a week located on a little French island. European men who could speak English made out the best. Sometimes a girl would have to argue with the conductor about cashing a traveler's check. The gallant European would then move in and make the translation. He would then have an excuse to sit next to you for a long train ride."

Vending Machines

Modern technology has not yet developed to the point whereby you obtain romance through a vending machine; but be aware of possibilities adjacent to vending machines. Keep plenty of change in your pocket or purse. People are forever dependent

104

upon somebody else to make change for them so they can operate a vending machine or parking meter. Why not ask an interesting looking stranger for change, or be prepared to give change? Once you have done a small favor for a person, the ground has been laid for building a conversation.

Write a Celebrity

Perhaps there is a local television personality, an author, or sports figure for whom your libido overflows. Assume further that you know nobody who can fix you up with that person. Why not write that person, giving an honest statement of your intentions? Also include some background information about yourself and a photograph. True, national celebrities of both sexes receive more unsolicited social invitations than they can possibly process. Your local hero or heroine, on the other hand, may be in the market for some new social life. There is nothing illegal or immoral about writing a public figure. Following up the letter with a phone call can pay dividends.

Timid and socially inhibited, you might feel self-conscious about such a direct approach. One less assertive variation of the same technique is to extend the celebrity you are trying to cultivate an invitation to a party. An unattached insurance woman started a romance with the local business columnist by extending him an invitation to an open house at her insurance agency.

Zoos

Women who prefer divorced men with children should be prepared for impromptu encounters at the local zoo. Help that lonely divorced young father untangle the balloon string entwined around a button on his child's coat. If your child starts talking to another child, check out the latter's parent. Cute little children sometimes have very interesting, unattached parents. What a unique story to tell your friends. "My romance with Fred began in a monkey house."

Chapter 6

SYSTEMATIC EFFORTS

"You have to create your own luck," say some of the luckiest people. Impromptu situations for meeting people sometimes fall right into your lap, but if you are not that fortunate you may have to help fate along. One major strategy for bringing sex, love, companionship, and fun into your life is to set up or place yourself in the right situations. Many people choose jobs, friends, sports, and even places to live for the primary purpose of meeting other people. Nobody should feel unworthy or unwanted because they apply systematic effort to finding a mate. Other people by the thousands gear much of their life toward finding people whether or not they admit it. Besides, don't you think you should put at least as much effort into finding a lover as finding a job?

This chapter provides you with an assortment of systematic efforts for meeting other people. All have one thing in common. Meeting people will be a byproduct of some other activity. You will not be spending money for the exclusive purpose of buying companionship (those methods are the subject of my next chapter). Although some of these systematic efforts will be familiar to you, even the most experienced lover will find something new in these pages.

What is the difference between the systematic efforts described in this chapter and the impromptu situations described in the last chapter? The main difference lies in the way you use them. For instance, a friend of mine had a sudden urge to smoke a cigarette. The nearest cigarette machine was in a

laundromat. In the process of purchasing ciga-
rettes, he discovered a new romance—an impromptu situation. However, if my friend had visited that laundromat for the primary purpose of
picking up a girl, the laundromat would have to
be classified as a systematic effort.

Whether you meet a new friend through serendipity or by careful planning, you still have to
stay alert to the possible romantic opportunities
in the situation.

Alcoholics Anonymous

Helen Gurley Brown and other advisors to
women have suggested prospecting for men at Alcoholics Anonymous. Join a chapter in a neighborhood where the type of men that interest you probably live. By the time most men (or women) have
joined AA, they have ruined relationships with
their present spouses. You may be the support they
need to compensate for their present loss of love
and alcohol.

One attractive, intelligent girl from Atlanta
stopped drinking through AA. She claims that
when in a strange city, a local AA chapter provides her with "instant friendship." For both
drinkers and non-drinkers, AA is a passable way
of improving one's social life.

Alumnae Groups and Reunions

A college education is supposed to pay dividends for many years after graduation. One way of
collecting these dividends is to search for dates or
mates at alumnae clubs or class reunions. People
are open with old classmates; you might learn
about old friends who have split with their
spouses or are contemplating doing so.

A disadvantage of class reunions is that you

meet people mostly of your own age. If you like older men or younger women, try your luck elsewhere. A few colleges, such as Mount Holyoke, sponsor mixers for women who have been out ten years or less. An informant rates the calibre of men attending these mixers "above average."

Art Galleries and Shows

Wayne, a New York City lover of art and women, satisfies his taste for both by attending art galleries and shows. Newspapers list previews of openings which will help you schedule your prospecting. Art galleries and shows are sprinkled with other people playing the singles game. Both straight and gay reap social benefits from their interest in art.

A word of caution. Learn something about the artist or artists on display before your hunting expedition. More knowledge about art is required to prospect at galleries and shows than at art museums.

Bait Method

Helen Gurley Brown advises the single girl to use "bait" to catch men. Men can play the same game. Wear or carry something that evokes conversation from strangers. Carry a bird cage, a cello, a set of skis in July, scuba diving equipment in February, a ventriloquist dummy, or a Raggedy Ann doll.

Joan hit upon the bait method while on a diet. Working in a hospital, Joan felt obliged to take two coffee breaks each day. She has an aversion to coffee without cream and sugar—two items forbidden by her diet. As a substitute, she drank water at coffee breaks for the duration of her diet. For reasons I never understood, Joan decided to carry around a urine specimen container for her water. Four different men she had not talked to previously began conversations with her that week.

Bank Club

In Texas they have come up with a method of changing the standard arrangement on checking accounts from "ex-dividend" to "sex-dividend." To attract up and coming singles as depositors, this bank arranged a variety of singles activities including parties and cruises. Maybe something like this exists in your area.

Hank, the bachelor banker who brought me this information, has been trying to move his conservative institution in this direction. Hank's suggestions so far have received a lukewarm reaction. In the interim, he is contemplating conducting a survey among single girls in his area to determine if they would be interested in joining such a club.

Beaches

Beaches work best for teeny boppers and young adults. Physique is more important at beaches than psyche. Physically attractive girls cannot avoid finding male companionship at beaches if they follow this simple plan. Wear a suntan and brief bathing suit. Lie down on one side of a large blanket and conspicuously read a book with "Sex" in the title. (Even this book should work wonders.)

Beaches, more so than any other public place, are designed for pick-ups. The larger public beaches are meeting havens for both heterosexuals and homosexuals. Lonely straight and gay people alike can be seen roaming public beaches. Bring along suntan oil and a list of opening lines.

Blind Dates

You do not have to be desperate to date someone you have never met before. Three percent of adults, according to a survey conducted by one of my research associates, met their spouse on an absolute blind date. When you move into a new town, blind dates can be particularly effective. Ask everybody you feel comfortable asking, for a few prospects. Call the prospect directly and arrange a meeting. Directness of this sort works better than having the intermediary arrange a meeting between the two of you. Here is a useful telephone technique:

"Hello, may I please speak to Marge Baxter?"

"This is Marge speaking."

"May I call you Marge? A friend of yours, Annette Stanton, suggested that I call you. I'm new in town. Annette and I work together. I'm a chemist."

"Oh yes, I know Annette."

"My purpose in calling is to make an arrangement to meet you. Annette told me that you are a delightful person. May I tell you something about myself?"

Blind dates give you a chance to capitalize on the *ripple effect*. Assume that you are starting from scratch in your social contacts. Your blind date might invite you to a party where you could meet some new friends. Gradually your circle of friends, acquaintances, and dates enlarges. A ripple of this nature is sometimes better than trying to make a big social splash.

Bridge Classes and Tournaments

Bridge players are more interested in bridge than in people when playing cards. Bridge tournaments, even more so than bridge classes, have a stark social atmosphere. Never, ever ask a bridge player a social question while he or she is playing a hand or pondering a bid. Many serious bridge players advise strongly against bridge and sex partnership with the same person. Keep these admonitions in mind should you want to play the singles game in a bridge setting.

Bridge settings are only good for prospecting if you are emotionally involved with bridge. Bridge players of tournament caliber hate, despise, loathe, and scorn people who enter bridge tournaments for fun. Should my conclusion sound harsh to you, visit a local bridge tournament. While you are there, keep this tip in mind. Complimenting a bridge player on his or her bridge skill is a more effective relationship builder than reacting to his or her appearance or personality. Helen is trying to capture the attention of a male bridge player during a tournament. See the different results she gets with the first and second approach:

1. "My, that is a stunning looking sweater you're wearing."

"What the hell are you talking about? Why are you bothering me?"

2. My, that is a stunning way you played that last hand."

"Say, you're pretty smart. Stick around. Maybe we can get together at 2 A.M. when play is through for the day."

Brokerage Houses

A collection of financially well-off people—ninety percent of whom are male—congregate every business day at downtown locations open to the public. Furthermore, there is a steady turnover of people. Stock brokerage offices thus provide a unique opportunity for women to prospect for males. Men can play the game to a lesser extent.

Wealthy widows sometimes watch stock transaction tapes.

Noon hours are ideal for watching stockmarket watchers, but you might make an earlier visit before all the best prospects are taken. One natural opener for the boardroom is, "How do you think the market will finish?" Airline stocks are unpredictable and thus a good conversation topic.

Don't be disappointed if some of the stock addicts you try to pick up behave like bridge addicts. But isn't a potentially profitable addiction better for your mental health?

Business Banquets

Ruth keeps herself supplied with men by attending business banquets. Usually the ratio is 90 males to 10 females at these affairs. How does Ruth get invited to these banquets? She doesn't. Ruth relies upon a connection of hers at a hotel to inform her when banquets are scheduled.

Ruth arrives before the banquet guests are seated. Many guests at that time congregate at the bar. Prospecting is sometimes better after the banquet. Unattached men usually notice an available woman in a hotel setting. Every normal male fantasizes that while visiting a hotel he might make a quick score. Should hit and run not be your game, don't be discouraged. Few men expect to act out their every fantasy.

Causes (Particularly Women's Lib)

Joining a cause is an effective way of meeting people. Pick the cause of your choice; but all things being equal, pick a cause which attracts the type of people (sex and life style) you are interested in meeting.

Women's liberation groups, such as your local

chapter of National Organization for Women (NOW), are useful for meeting educated, assertive, and alert women. Many liberationists are young and single. Some are married. Others have split from husbands who cannot tolerate a self-sufficient gal who wants equal status.

Before signing up for NOW, do your homework about Women's Lib. Should you have no sympathy for their aims, flee before they catch on to you. Once your true intent in coming to the meetings—treating women as sex objects—is discovered, the most polite thing you will be called is "male chauvinist pig."

When trying to cultivate a feminist, disregard all those bad jokes about liberated women being offended by male courtesies. Continue to open car doors, pay for dinner, and help her on with her coat unless she asks you to do otherwise. Liberated women want to be treated equal to males on *important matters* such as intellectual respect and job opportunities.

What about feminist attitudes toward sex? Providing she doesn't feel sexploited, a feminist, similar to most intelligent and assertive women, should be a terrific sex partner—you may never have the need to pursue another cause (unless *she* finds somebody else).

Churches

Should normal, well-adjusted, conservative types suit your fancy, try church as a hunting ground. Although church attendance has shown a decline, about 30 percent of Christians still attend church. Besides, you might be looking for the "wholesome god-fearing type" who *does* attend regularly. Regular members score better than the occasional visitor. After a while the reverend or priest might even introduce you to other unattached parishioners. Females are in larger supply than males at church.

Unitarian churches give careful thought to the well being of unattached adults. Ex-members of all religions feel comfortable at Unitarian gatherings, many of whom are divorced or separated. Sunday coffee and donut breakfasts at Unitarian meetings are geared for people prospecting. Dan, a divorced college professor, notes, "I never thought I would have to resort to going to church to meet women, but the Unitarian church has really helped me get back into the singles scene."

Clubs, Organizations and Associations

Lonely? Let your fingers do the prospecting through the yellow pages. You will find a wide array of clubs and associations that you can join for a modest fee listed in the yellow pages of any big city telephone directory. A few visits will convince you that the real purpose of many of these clubs is for unattached people to find companionship. Many computer dating companies advertise under the club section of the yellow pages. One advantage of a social club is that you need no interest other than in meeting people to join.

The effectiveness of these clubs as a source of supply for sex, love, and companionship varies considerably. Begin by choosing a club that reflects your interests. Philatelists, mountain climbers, chess players, bridge players, camera fans, and book lovers can all find a club to match their interests. One or two meetings at the club (or better yet, *clubs)* you choose will give you some indication of its social value to you.

Displaying genuine interest in the central activities of the club will increase your attractiveness to other members. Here is an example of what not to do:

Fred ventured to a camera club to attend a meeting on underwater photography. He left after ten minutes. During the next meeting (which featured a discussion about nude photography) Fred engaged Sue, another member, in conversation. Asked by Sue why he left so early last time, Fred replied, "Oh, there just wasn't anybody interesting looking at that meeting." Sue, an authentic camera enthusiast, walked away from Fred, thus terminating his chances of getting a relationship started.

Clubs and associations can be used to meet people of all ages. Some of the loneliest people in our society—senior citizens—are using their local chapter of the Golden Age Club to improve their social life. Lonely older men can also be found at chess clubs.

Country clubs are an expensive and ineffective way to meet unattached people. Despite the still glamorous ring to the term "country club," most are populated by older, married golf players. A handful of bridge playing widows can also be found. Tennis and swim clubs have bypassed country clubs as a meeting place for younger people.

Tom, a black urban planner, tells how he uses the best known club of all to prospect for women.

"That's right, I said the YWCA, the women's branch of the Y. My job requires extensive travel. Whenever I'm in a strange town, I sit down in the lobby of the local YWCA. Sure, it looks a little suspicious, but I explain to the clerk at the desk that I'm waiting for somebody. When I see a couple of girls talking in the lobby, I join their conversation. Some of my best girlfriends, white and black, have come into my life through this method. It makes much more sense than heading for the nearest bar to pick up a girl."

Colleges and Universities

Why invest from $8,000 to $15,000 in something without receiving fringe benefits? Choose your college for both social and academic reasons. Check the male-female ratio before deciding upon a school. For instance, Purdue University is great for finding a husband. You may know of other top-rated schools that have a five to one male to female ratio, but there is a "can't miss" something about that venerable old Indiana institution. Rose, an average-looking first year graduate student in chemistry, received three proposals at Purdue before spring recess.

Maybe you have already attended college, or can only attend part-time. Do not be discouraged. Part-time students also participate in the sexual largesse of schools. Take courses where the male-female ratio works in your favor. Women might take accounting or investment courses. Men might take contemporary literature courses. Almost every college has an evening program that may also provide some good leads for social life.

Don't expect to find wealthy men attending evening classes. Most night students are attending classes in order to advance in their jobs. The corporate hot shots and professional men have already achieved the formal education they need to advance.

Look for prospective mates both in and outside the classroom. Before leaving campus, make a routine visit to the coffee shop or recreational hall. Course registration time offers some terrific possibilities. Sally, an artful operator in these matters, works as a secretary in the business department of a college. She volunteers to tend the registration desk for her department. During the three day registration period, at least three hundred men have to come to her asking for information. What better odds can a girl ask for?

College lawns are esthetic as well as functional. Visit the nearest college lawn during the first warm days of spring. You will find both men and women in a relaxed social mood. Medical school lawns have more coeds than dandelions. Unattached girls drape these lawns hoping to catch the attention of a medical student.

Concerts

Outdoor concerts have an edge over indoor concerts for people meeting. Outdoors or indoors, the best strategy is to attend a concert that will attract the type of person you are trying to meet. Waiting in line to enter the concert sometimes presents splendid people-meeting opportunities. Come armed with some information at your fingertips about the singer, group, or orchestra featured.

Darryl, a pop concert fan, uses this opener while waiting in line, "What do you girls know about the rumor that——are going to split as a group after this performance?" Confirmed, or unconfirmed, Darryl will still sound impressive because of his inside information.

Conventions

Unconventional behavior takes place at conventions. Many people would continue to attend conventions if all the speakers, technical papers presented, or products displayed were cancelled. Hometown puritans become sexually liberated once caught in a whirl of conventional morality.

Armed with this information, you will know how to interpret most romantic statements levelled at you at conventions. Caution: Call girls and prostitutes follow the convention circuit to ease the suffering of those men who can't score on a non-fee basis.

Despite the one night stand mentality that pervades them, some good relationships can be initiated at conventions. Where else might a girl find so many professional or businessmen concentrated in one spot? Professional and businesswomen also have their own conventions. Some conventions such as the American Psychological Association or the Personnel and Guidance Association are well supplied with both sexes.

Simply be visible at the convention. Purchase (usually about three dollars), find, or make up your own badge. Convention groups do not hire detectives to eject people traveling under false credentials. Do you think the Eastern Podiatry Association cares if you attend some of their meetings to find a loose podiatrist? Do you think the American Home Economics Association is concerned that you are not really a male home economist? All your badge claims is that you have a name and hometown.

Courses and Lessons

Courses other than those taken for college credit can help along your social life. Pick your course according to the male-female odds you want and the type of people you are interested in meeting. Mary Ann, a resourceful girl from Pittsburgh, navigated herself into a beautiful relationship by taking flying lessons. In addition to finding the number one man in her life, she developed a few more casual relationships.

Gourmet cooking classes, golf lessons, language schools, Karate and Judo schools, and so forth can teach you skills and improve your personal life at the same time. People often reveal a lot about themselves while taking lessons. If that prospect curses, stomps his feet, and hurls verbal abuse at innocent bystanders when his crepe burns, he will put on a repeat performance in your kitchen.

Investment classes given by stock brokerage firms are free and are usually attended by younger people with above average incomes. If money is important to you, proceed accordingly.

Dances (Private)

Private dances such as that annual hospital Christmas party can be a very effective way of meeting people. (In the next chapter we'll talk about public dances for singles.) Even the most over-protective date cannot openly object if you dance with a stranger. Do not feel self-conscious if you attend a private dance unescorted; it may facilitate your meeting new people. Everybody attending the dance either belongs to the sponsoring organization or is a member's guest. Either way, it provides a comfortable way to begin a conversation.

Women can get a lot of social mileage out of their club or company dance. Invite a man you really want to spend time with. Inviting somebody to your dance is a nice way of saying, "You are a person I'm proud to be seen with."

Dog Shows

Somebody has spread the word that dog lovers are also good people lovers. This may or may not be true. People who show dogs are almost fanatical about them; during the show they have eyes only for canines. Nevertheless, if you are looking for diversity in your pursuit of companionship, attend a dog show. Complimenting a person's show dog gives that person a giant ego boost. Try turning on a dog fancier with, "How do you ever manage to keep him (check out the sex carefully, dog lovers are sensitive) in such beautiful shape?"

Discussion Groups

Check the local happenings section of your newspaper. People meet in small groups to discuss a wide variety of topics including books, drugs, politics, and sex. Don't be concerned if the topic of the night leaves you cold. Discussion groups generally turn into rap sessions about almost anything. While somebody is rapping, listen carefully. You can learn pretty fast whether or not he or she is worth pursuing. Tony, the old-fashioned he-man (male chauvinistic by today's standards) type, made his move toward a girl after he heard her express these attitudes in a discussion group about the American male: "I pity the poor man of today. He works so hard and so many women don't show him any appreciation. If I had a husband, I would treat him like a king. When he came home at night, he would really be in store for a treat."

Discussion groups are often collecting places for lonely people in search of partners. Give it a try. Even if you don't find a friend, you might find some intellectual stimulation.

Exotic Happenings

A few people fall upon exotic ways to meet people. San Francisco's "Tuesday Downtown Operators and Observors," a bachelor club that exists to wine and dine the city's most beautiful girls, is one example. For one quarter of a century, an ever-changing group of swinging bachelors have been inviting three or four girls at a time to lunch with over 60 eligible bachelors.

The "Vice Dean" of TDO is assigned the task of uncovering three or four beautiful girls for lunch every Tuesday. Potential guests are stopped on airplanes, elevators, and the street. Every luncheon guest puts her name and phone number in a register, and is given the name and phone number of all the TDO's she met. Twice a year all luncheon guests are invited back for a grand party where males again outnumber the females.

The system works. All types of relationships, including marriage, stem from these luncheons and parties. Maybe you can find something on a lesser scale available to you in your city. If you are female, pretty, and live near San Francisco, why not send TDO your photo with a letter of introduction?

Fire Island

Fire Island is a fast-paced summer resort near Long Island that many singles inhabit, but it lacks the marriage bureau atmosphere of an actual singles resort. In season, one or two of the beaches are veritable mating grounds. Escapees from the pressures of New York City roam the beaches looking for action. Heterosexuals and homosexuals frequent the island and its many bars. Fire Island, or other resorts like them, work best for the young swinger. You need a good line of patter and a large capacity for drugs or alcohol to make the scene in a big way at such places.

Before investing your people-meeting funds on Fire Island, read Burt Hirschfeld's novel by the same name. People who have been there say it's as good (or as bad, depending upon your interests) as Hirshchfeld describes.

Folk Dancing

If you enjoy folk or square dancing, you will probably dig folk and square dancers. Such people are less phony than the people you will meet at singles bars or resorts. Spend some time at developing friendships before you conclude that there is no action around. Square dancers are the type of people who, although friendly, will need to trust you before introducing you to their friends.

Friends

Referrals through friends are still the best way of meeting mates and dates. Fifty percent of married people met their mate through introduction by a friend. Take the initiative. Systematically ask all your friends if they might introduce you to somebody. Women are generally better matchmakers than men. If you are self-confident enough to swallow a little pride, ask old lovers to help you with your social life.

Women sometimes use male homosexuals as a source of leads for dates. Gay males are usually sensitive enough to understand what a woman is looking for in a man. You can return the favor by going on men-hunting safaris together.

Cultivate single platonic friends. Unattached people of the opposite sex are the best source of referral. People married for a long time may be too far removed from the singles game to recognize what type of person you are seeking. Larry, a sales manager, is a case in point:

"I'm through asking married people for leads. Here I am 32 and divorced after nine years of marriage. My friends fix me up with a separated housewife with three kids. Who needs that? My ex-wife is a housewife with three kids. I want to swing a little."

How can one avoid the agony of spending an entire evening in a zero rapport situation? Have your friends introduce you over cocktails, coffee, or at a party. Should you and the referral click, you can spend the rest of the evening (or the night) together. Should you and your referral be a mismatch, only an hour or so of this social calamity need be suffered.

Fund Drives

Much more than money can be collected at fund drives. Volunteer to be on the fund-raising committee of your local art gallery, or join the United Fund staff (if you can fight your way past all the do-gooders who are trying to impress their bosses by joining). Proceed then to call everybody you would like to date, who hasn't yet asked you. After giving your pitch for money, shift the conversation to easier topics. One good opener is, "Okay, I'm through with the gory part of my phone call, how have you been?"

Gay Liberation Front

GLF offers you the advantages of both a club and a cause in meeting partners for sex, love, companionship and fun. Male and female homosexuals constitute 99 percent of the membership, and the remaining one percent are at least gay sympathizers. Should you be gay, lonely, well educated and bright, I would strongly recommend GLF over gay bars as a place to prospect for a mate. Tim, a college senior, commented, "Once GLF came to campus, I finally had a place to meet men. Nobody puts me down because of the way I think, dress, or talk."

Grapevine

Once you become unattached, tell all your divorced, separated and widowed friends about your situation. Magically, this news will travel on the formerly married *grapevine*. If the grapevine works in your favor, you will begin to receive invitations to attend parties and other social gatherings from people you never knew before. Marjorie confessed, "Right after I split, I head for the telephone. For three nights I call everybody I know and gently mention that I'm now on the market again. It takes a lot of phone calls to make a few connections, but it is worth it."

Halloween

Jill, a physically well-endowed divorcée with three children, went trick or treating to best advantage; she steered her children toward the doors of available men. Dressed in a leopard costume, Jill was indeed a Halloween surprise. Dates with two different men resulted from this unusual maneuver. Caution: Take off your mask, once invited in for a cookie or drink. Few people will ask for the phone number of a masked stranger.

Hotel Lobbies

People finding can be quite good in hotel lobbies. Jan carries a set of postcards with her on every trip: "My technique is amazingly good. I sit down in a conspicuous place and begin to write out some postcards. This gives a man a good excuse for starting a conversation with me. Just sitting there would make me look like a prostitute."

Ralph has a version of the hotel technique used

by many other traveling businessmen. "When I check into a new town, I find out which hotels are populated by stewardesses. Usually they are close to the airport. I spend time in those hotel cocktail lounges, or I camp right in the lobby. It is time well invested because I make regular trips to the same cities. If stewardesses know I'll be making return visits, they are more willing to give me a chance."

Japanese Restaurant

Japanese restaurant owners have come up with a pleasant way of combining people prospecting with dining. Inquire about the facilities at your local "Japanese Tea House," or similarly named restaurant. Places of this type have tables for eight. Customers postpone eating until the table of eight is filled. As a result, you meet new people. The informality and private dining room atmosphere encourages conversation among the diners.

Esther, a petite Jewish gal, looks Japanese. Inevitably, when attending a tea house, somebody will gingerly ask, "I take it you are Japanese." Esther replies, "No, I'm Jewish." Laughter, in response to her comment, immediately breaks down communication barriers. Esther has found a method of meeting men that works particularly well for her.

Jobs and Careers

The grandest people-finding strategy of all is to work in jobs or pursue careers that are heavily populated by people of the opposite sex. Girls, if you like numbers and figures, take up accounting as a profession. In 1990 there may be an equal number of male and female accountants. For now, over ninety percent of accountants are male.

Frank cares more about social life than high income. During the summer he works as a social director on cruise ships. During the balance of the year, dapper Frank works as a high school social studies teacher. Says Frank: What a way to live. Every year or so we get a new supply of sharp young female teachers in my school. It's like being a well-paid college senior for the rest of your life. A man can't miss as a high school teacher in a big central school."

Males do not have a monopoly on bolstering their social life through teaching. Bernadine has a job teaching school at an Army base. "When I'm too old to attract the new lieutenants, I'll look for a divorced colonel to marry. In the meantime, I'll continue doing my duty for my country.

Glamor jobs—those that put you into favorable contact with the public—are outstanding for elevating your social life. If you are a movie producer, the director of a modeling agency, a starlet, an international airline stewardess, a racing car driver, or the Executive Vice President of Playboy Enterprises, you won't even need to read this book.

Laundromats

Wash your clothing and do your magazine reading in a laundromat located in a singles neighborhood. Attesting to the value of this method are urban laundromats that cater to singles. Refreshments are served to enhance the casual meeting atmosphere. Do lots of wash. A key to success in any public place is to become a regular. A familiar face overcomes the paranoid attitude that many big city dwellers have about strangers. Wear what is *de rigueur* for laundromats. Faded clothing, slightly worn sweaters or similar attire makes you look legitimate in a laundromat.

Ask for change, comment upon magazines, help others sort their wash, and review those conversation openers suitable for washday mentioned in the last chapter.

Parks

Sara combines her interest in art with her interest in meeting men, to make clever use of public parks. She brings her easel, paint and brushes to a populated section of the parks and waits for men to come her way. You may not want to have an affair with every art admirer you encounter, but you will at least meet a range of prospects.

Feeding pigeons, sleeping on benches, pitching horseshoes, drinking wine from a bottle in a bag, or walking a vicious looking dog are ineffective ways to use parks for meeting people. Flying a kite, taking pictures with an expensive camera, walking a pussy cat or small dog, or riding a tandem bicycle with the back seat empty are much more effective approaches.

Parties

Serious people hunters never refuse an invitation to a party. Parties provide the ideal opportunity for meeting unattached people (or people who are contemplating becoming unattached). Everybody at a party has license to talk to everybody else. Equally important, it is socially acceptable to move away from somebody when you are bored or see another more promising situation.

Cocktail parties are better for people meeting than are sit-down dinners. Sitting in one place sets up an entrapment that decreases your number of contacts. Parties for couples and singles are four times as effective as singles mixers. Why? However you rationalize it, there is an undercurrent of

128

desperation about being at a singles party. In contrast, it is socially smart or cool to be unattached at a mixed party.

"Reject parties" were popular for a while. Allow Bonnie to explain: "We did these in Washington a few years back. Say, I would throw the party and invite ten girls. Each girl would have to bring one man she used to date but is no longer interested in. Thus we all had a chance to meet each other's rejects. Some of the fellows got wise and became indignant about it."

Bruncheon parties give you an opportunity to invite people with social calendars so tight that they might turn down your Friday or Saturday night invitation. You can even ask celebrities to Sunday bruncheons and expect a positive reply. Invite that bachelor congressman from your district to your next bruncheon. What about that sharp looking consumer affairs adviser you have seen on TV? Maybe she is eager to meet one of her admirers.

Parties given by you lead to some pleasant reciprocal invitations. Sometimes the best way to get the ripple effect going for you is to throw a party. Be unique. Give your party in February—a time of the year when most people receive few party invitations. You then have a better chance of the people you really want to attend accepting your invitation.

Petitions

Yolanda, an unattached female who works in the front office of an apartment complex, receives my gold cup for the most innovative (and practicable) method of meeting men. During a two month period she invested two nights a week obtaining signatures on a petition "to request a shopping cen-

129

ter in our neighborhood." Who could object to such a legitimate sounding proposal? Yolanda knocked on the doors of married people, single females, and single males. Yolanda recognized that if she only polled unattached males she would become the local legend. Ten evenings of petitioning provided Yolanda with all the men she could handle.

What cause can you petition for in your neighborhood? All you need to get started is a cause, a clipboard, and a few sharp pencils.

Picnics

Attend all the picnics you can, but expect the people-picking to be slimmer than at indoor parties. Picnics are mostly family affairs. Office picnics (maybe they will come back in a big way someday) offer some interesting possibilities. Divorced and separated people like picnics for their children, thus making the picnic route more promising. Picnics, like parties, make it easy for anybody to converse with a stranger. If an inspired opener doesn't come to mind, try this: "What do you know about that bed of poison ivy in the woods?"

Political Organizations

Assuming you feel equipped to compete with the horde of mate-hunters already there, join a political organization for social purposes. As Pete, a state senator, explains it, "Those campaign helpers are terrific. Sure, they are coming here mostly to meet men. Some men come here to meet women. But they also do a damn good job of keeping their party in power. What the hell can you expect? They deserve something for their efforts. We can't offer them money."

Develop a strategy to maintain an edge over the

130

competition. Get involved in local political organizations during the off years when few people volunteer to help. Work for Democrats one half the year and for Republicans the next. Choose political groups in neighborhoods that are populated by the type of people you hope to meet.

Relocate Geographically

"No good men are left in New York, just a bunch of phonies, mama's boys, wolves, and queers," said a disappointed single. Should you sympathize with this type of thinking (it could be said of any town in which you are lonely), try geographic relocation. Before taking the plunge, check the latest census figures of the town you have in mind. At this writing Washington D.C. is oversupplied with females, while almost any mining town and most cities in Alaska have an oversupply of men.

Before leaving your friends, family and job, ask yourself, "Is it me or the town that prevents me from having a good social life?"

Residence Halls

Although fading in popularity, residences for women are worth exploring. Capitalize upon any opportunity to date a girl who lives under such an arrangement. Arrive early and wait in the lobby. Since you have a legitimate reason for waiting there, it will soften the lecherous man's image you might otherwise project.

College dormitories, including their dining halls, are a similar hunting ground. Larry uses a technique that he claims has provided him with some good relationships: "I ask around in the lobby if anybody upstairs would be interested in going to the movies with a stranger. You may not find the campus queen rushing down the stairs to meet you.

131

I don't care, I'm not the campus king either.

Roof Tops

Roof tops are in for worshippers of sun and fun. During summer months, many young people are finding each other on these havens in the sky. Modern high rise apartment buildings provide the most action, but in Boston (and probably other large cities) brownstones are used as beaches. Gordon, a management consultant working in an office building on Boylston Street in Boston, noticed the roof top festivities a few floors below him. One lunch hour, dressed in his business suit, Gordon paid a visit to the roof top across the way. "I was pleasantly surprised. Instead of telling me to go away the fellows and girls were friendly. They gave me a beer and told me to come back tomorrow with my bathing suit. I did. That's how I met Betty. She and I might become a permanent couple."

Sensitivity Groups

Hundreds of new couples are meeting each other in sensitivity groups, couples groups, and marathon therapy groups. Groups of this nature tell you more about another person in one or two sessions than you might learn in two months of dating. Under the emotional support and comfort of these groups people will openly discuss their major hang-ups. Also, they may tell you what they are really looking for in a relationship. Comments such as those given by Earl and Jean are not uncommon:

Earl: "What really bugged me about my wife was that she used sex as a prize. If I did things that pleased her, such as taking her mother shopping, she would have sex with me. If she didn't like something, even the dumbest little thing like tracking mud in the house, she would avoid me like I had V.D."

Jean: "What I can't handle about Al is that he won't react to anything. I tell him my period is five days late, and he says, 'So.' I tell him that our relationship is going bad, and he asks me if he left his fishing tackle box at my apartment. I swear, tomorrow I am going to tell him we're through and see if he says anything."

Why are couples groups good for meeting people? One reason many people join couples groups is that they are contemplating splitting and need some encouragement from others. One woman complained that encounter groups were breaking up dozens of marriages in her town. What she didn't realize is that these were couples that had been wanting to split for years. Groups of this nature give you a chance to meet some unattached people freshly on the singles market.

Sports

Sports present many splendid impromptu situations for finding people, as described in the last chapter. Sports can also be approached systematically as a way of meeting people. Spectacularly successful in this regard are ski clubs. Members of such clubs, according to some fascinating research, are as much interested in meeting new people as they are in skiing. The more elaborate of these clubs arrange for faraway ski trips, barbecues, and summer travel. Club members are mostly single, under thirty, and physically healthy. (As you athletes already know, physically healthy people make good sex partners!)

As told by the director of my ski club research team, "I met my fiancee at this ski club, and many other people have been just as lucky."

Spouses (Friends of)

Forward thinkers about to terminate their marriages cultivate relationships with friends of their spouses. For instance, your husband's business acquaintance may be just the type of man you are looking for. Or he may have a friend who fits your taste in men.

Recently separated women generally find a willing supply of studs among their husband's friends. Sally's comments are oft-repeated by other women:

"What a dumb son-of-a-bitch Bill's golfing buddy turned out to be. He calls me one morning at the house offering to help me out over the rough spots until I got my social life going again. The rough spots he had in mind weren't my feelings but my sex drive. He offered to screw me whenever I felt the need for sex. The jerk suggested that we could meet at a hotel room on Thursday mornings. He didn't even mention taking me to breakfast or lunch."

Stores

Stores can also be used for people shopping. Pat, a long-haired, over-grown teenager finds her men by hanging around automotive speed shops. Sometimes she buys a can of crankcase additive or some chrome bolts just to prevent the proprietor from accusing her of loitering. Pat has almost no competition in the speed shop. Very few girls shop for men or auto parts in these stores.

Gigolos sometimes ply their trade by lingering around expensive shops in larger cities. Wealthy, quite often lonely, housewives and widows frequent such places.

Large book stores have a casual, relaxed atmosphere conducive to picking up strangers. Younger intellectual types do some of their people finding in bookstores, but they are less systematic about it than gigolos.

Survey Taking

Survey taking for the real purpose of meeting people is sometimes effective, but it can be risky. Suspicious women may report you to the police or Better Business Bureau. Men are less prone to turn in suspicious-looking women. Bruce, an enterprising young woman hunter, explains how this method works: "I pick out a neighborhood where a lot of girls live. I put on my best suit and carry an attaché case. I knock on each door. If a man or an uninteresting looking girl answers, I say, 'Pardon me, I'm taking a survey. Do you own your own refrigerator? Thank you.' If a nice-looking girl answers the door, I begin to ask a lot of questions.

There

Go *there*. Anyplace he or she might be, simply go there and make yourself visible. If the type of girls you want to meet cavort in hospital cafeterias, hang around hospital cafeterias. Should men who watch wrestling matches intrigue you, sit ringside in the wrestling arena *sans* escort. He will find you. Should lawyers suit your taste in men, hang around the courtroom on your lunch hour or get assigned to jury duty (you'll have two weeks to sit around and prospect for a lawyer while serving your country).

Travel

Author Jean Baer reports how travel can be used exclusively for the purpose of man-finding. A friend of hers travels the 8 A.M. New York City to Washington air shuttle just to meet men. Considerable time and money are consumed in such an effort, but how can you put a price tag on finding one good executive husband or lover?

Weddings

Weddings are another natural place to meet people. Almost every unattached person at a wedding is neutral or favorable toward matrimony. Romance pervades the air and a wedding ceremony titillates you with the splendor of falling in love.

Remarriage wedding ceremonies, although less elaborate than first marriage ceremonies, also have a romantic appeal. Besides, what better way to hint to 47 year old Harry that marriage is not only for youngsters.

Chapter 7

COMMERCIAL METHODS

Sex, love, companionship, and fun can be bought as well as found. Specifically, you can purchase the chance to meet people. What kind of relationship develops after the initial contact is your responsibility. Let's assume that so far no fortuitous impromptu situation has come your way and that you want to begin doing something constructive about your social life. Like any other business, the "mating trade" (to use author John Godwin's term) has some good and some poor services.

My general advice is to buy sex, love, companionship, and fun only after you have exhausted the non-commercial approaches. Nevertheless, investing a few dollars (or even a few thousand) in your personal life is a more pleasant alternative than loneliness. Many more people than those who openly admit it, have found their mate through the mating trade.

Apartment Houses for Singles

Landlords can help you improve your social life. Concentrated in the far west and south the singles-only apartment house or complex has become a popular method of meeting people. The premium in rent you pay over comparable luxury apartments is negligible. Required for survival in such a living arrangement is a lack of concern for privacy or individuality. As Anne describes it, "I met a lot of fellows, but they were mostly the noisy clown types. You almost felt forced into some mixer activities every free hour."

A well-worded classified ad is a potent way of locating unattached people interested in meeting you. No other investment for less than ten dollars can come close to furnishing you so many leads. After the newspaper mails back the replies your ad drew, the fun begins. This classified advertisement brought in 97 responses after running only one day in the Sunday edition of a medium-size city newspaper:

MALE, divorced doctor, new in town, age 43. Interested in meeting woman who enjoys dining, conversation, boating. Send full details about self.

Replies came from night cashiers to social workers with master's degrees. Fifteen of the letters indicated their zodiac sign. Two women volunteered to take the divorced doctor on a tour of their town. Several letters only gave classified box numbers (they too were advertising for companionship). A few other letters were sensuous in tone. For instance, "I'm sure you'll like me if you try me."

Flo, produced the most interesting reply:

HC 77641,

Your ad captured my attention and made me want to learn more about you.

I'm a writer, have auburn hair, green eyes, am 5′6″, 124 pounds, 31-years-old, live in the _____ section and work in _____. Some of my interests are swimming, boating, the theater and, of course, good communication with a man.

Hope to hear from you soon.

Sincerely,

Flo

Georgette gave the shortest reply:

Please call _____ after 8 P.M.

Thank you,

Georgette

Carol gave the most depressing reply:

Dear divorced doctor:

I have never done anything like this before, but today I was reading the newspaper and saw your ad. I said to myself, 'What have I got to lose even if I don't mail it? It did help to pass the lonely hours away.'

I am 40-years-old or young—it depends on how you look at it. Have red hair and I am 5'3" and weigh 121. I can't say what I really want in a man because I've been out of circulation for the last three years with a divorce. Since you are also divorced, you know how ugly and bad a divorce can make you feel.

I live in the north part of the city with my two cats. My phone number is _____ just in case you will be good enough to call me. I am home most of the time, so you are free to call anytime of the day.

Till I hear from you,

Carol

What happens when a girl with desirable credentials places an ad in the personals section of that same newspaper in that same city? One ad brought in 57 replies, suggesting that it also pays for a woman to advertise if she needs some leads for social life.

DIVORCÉE, age 28, art teacher, newcomer to town, wants to meet man for dancing, dining, conversation. Send details about self.

Replies poured in from some very impressive-sounding men. Included in the ranks of respondents were one physician, two college professors, one speech pathologist with a Ph.D. and many owners of small businesses. Answers also came from a 38 year old undergraduate biology major, a court clerk, an airlines clerk, and a 55 year old gentleman "between jobs." One computer dating outfit mailed the art teacher an application blank. One used car salesman encouraged a get-together in case she needed a new car. Five men expressed need for help with their painting. Surprisingly, nobody said anything that even the most uptight puritan would classify as pornographic or lewd. Men from early adulthood to social security retirees wanted a chance to date a 28 year old art teacher.

Dr. B.F.S., a college professor, came forth with the most intriguing letter:

Dear 1033 A—

Every other ad said "attractive"—so I'll assume that you are modest.

I'm an ex-football player, now a college professor and psychologist, never been married, but about 750½ unsuccessful affairs— and girlfriends always introduce me as, "the greatest guy I ever knew until I met you darling."

I live in a penthouse, drive a Toronado, spent last summer in China and Hawaii. I fish, swim, dance, dine, talk, and listen. I'm relatively good looking, articulate, sensitive, intelligent.

So if you would like, please call me at _____ or write _____.

Sincerely,
Bruce

Carlo wrote the shortest reply:

Hi, I am not much for *writing* so please call collect. Thanks, Carlo

A person who chose not to reveal his (conceivably *her*) name wrote the most pompous letter:

If you really live up to your ad I'm interested. I have the necessary qualifications you seek: * successful * sincere * charming, etc. etc. etc. Please phone _____ if not this letter will destruct by itself.

You might discover that newspapers in your area do not accept social ads. If so, go national. Several periodicals with a national or regional circulation print personal ads. Among these are the *New York Review of Books*, the *Village Voice*, and the *Los Angeles Free Press*. Here is an ad placed by a female in one of these publications.

ATTRACTIVE widow, age 30, one child, good sense of humor, intelligent, sensitive, sensual, creative professional, Boston. Where are stable not stodgy men, tall, attractive-looking professional or successful in arts, widowed, divorced, 35-40's, self-confident, interested in developing meaningful relationship, hiding?

A gentleman of highly specific tastes in women placed this ad in another national periodical:

TALL, non-charismatic, mobile, Chicago area bachelor, 35, seeks erratic, bizarre, slightly crazy female to re-ignite his zest for life and re-charge his battery.

Computer Dating

"Why be lonely anymore?" ask so many computer dating outfits in their advertisements. Originally started as a spoof by two college students, computer dating now operates in every medium or large city in the United States.

Present day divorce rates suggest that non-computer methods of matching up people have some serious flaws. Computer dating services have brought together many people who might otherwise not have met; but before filling out your computer companionship questionnaire, learn more about computer dating by reading Chapter 11.

Country Clubs for Singles

Year round country clubs are now in operation to help the unmarried and unconnected make the right social connection. Chateau D'Vie, one such club located in Rockland County near New York City, is in the process of branching out to other states. The singles country club represents the "total immersion technique" to making a connection. Yoga lessons, encounter groups, swimming, tennis, dancing, and (naturally) drinking are some of the featured attractions. Rounding out this club's appeal to the mating trade are bedrooms located on the premises. Reservations can be made in advance by weekenders and those people optimistic about finding a friendship that will be shared in a bedroom on the first night.

Janet, a 32 year old teacher, thinks a singles country club has some promise. "What can I tell you? It's not nearly as bad as the public meat market atmosphere of a big resort hotel. Everybody here is a member and you feel less awkward talking to another member than to some stranger. They offer you a lot of new 'in' things to do and most of the men are executives or professionals of some sort.

"I go up with my girlfriend. We have an unwritten agreement about finding men. If either of us find a fellow who looks sincere, we are on our own about where to spend the night. If we get hooked up with a loser, we can always say, 'I have to get back to my girlfriend.' "

Larry, a stockbroker, doesn't think the singles

country club is such a good investment. "I'm going to invest my sex dollars some place else. I may have picked a few losers by chance, but I think I see a pattern emerging. Broads joining this club think they are part of the country club set. They get uppity about the slightest thing. If they would lay the facts on the table and admit they are lonely and sad, I think they could start a more honest relationship with a man. Instead they lay all this phoney stuff on you about being here simply for the fresh air and recreational opportunities."

Dating Services

Vera, a lonely widow told me, "It's a national disgrace the way widows and divorced women are left with no way to find eligible men. I think the government should have a bureau where divorcées and widows can be introduced to proper gentlemen."

The Department of Health, Education, and Welfare does not yet have such a bureau—and it hasn't even been made a campaign promise—but commercial dating services are found in some cities. Dating services take you one important step beyond classified ads and the less expensive forms of computer dating. A representative from the service learns some important facts about you in an interview, including some impression of your attractiveness.

After your interview (and payment of fee) you are given at least one dozen referrals to pursue. Perhaps in the future, dating services will formally introduce you and your referral.

An advertisement for an established dating service calls it, "A beautiful way to meet beautiful people." Penny, a divorcée with four children who has sampled many commercial methods of meeting people says, "The _____ was not bad at all. I saw it advertised in the *Village Voice* and decided to give it a try. They were nice to me in the interview. Nine men called, and one man and I got along pretty well, although he does not really want to be tied down."

Cruises for Singles

Are you interested in taking a journey across the seas with a group composed mainly of middle-aged divorcées and widows? If your answer is affirmative, take a singles cruise. Some travel agents, recognizing that women want to meet men on these vacations, are careful not to overload any one cruise with females.

Eugene, a restaurant owner, provides a good example of the type of male who takes a singles cruise: "I'm a very busy man. I don't have much time for social life or chasing after women. When I need a rest or I want to meet some women, I take a vacation cruise. Money is no real problem for me. I meet enough women on a cruise to keep me happy for awhile."

Gigolos can be found on cruises. Young in appearance, and reasonably attractive, they are willing to invest in a cruise with the hopes of meeting a wealthy, older woman.

But, generally, at the worst, singles cruises are small artificial societies, where a group of lonely, anxious people are thrown together in search of companionship. People have been known to pack their bags at a stopping-off point, rather than endure the humiliation of the return trip.

At their best, singles cruises are a fair bargain. Allegedly, about seven percent of people who meet on a cruise marry each other within twelve months. In addition, unless you stay locked in your cabin, the chances of having a sexual experience with another warm, breathing human being are about 91 percent in your favor.

"Windjammer Cruises," and others like them are ideal for the physically robust. Singles populate these cruises aboard an impressive sailing yacht. Every shipmate on board is assigned a job befitting an old-fashioned sailor. A typical cruise might be a ten day sail to a Caribbean isle. Lois recounts her Windjammer days:

"I still have some bruises on my buttocks, but I got them in the line of duty. I made some permanent friendships on board. You can't miss. Everybody has to work together to survive. I met this hairy, muscular guy, who works as a real estate developer back in Boston. He has been a fantastic lover."

Coffee Houses

Singles use coffee houses to meet other singles, but couples also use coffee houses for dating purposes. Many mate seekers thus feel more comfortable hunting in coffee houses than in singles bars or public dances. Discotheque-styled coffee houses cater to the young, never-been-married set. The psychedelic lights and the sound decibel level at discotheques discourage the thirty and over crowd.

Coffee houses without music present good opportunities for finding serious, intellectual types. Avoid the highly commercialized, tourist places if you are seeking authentic hippie types, many of whom are turned off by alcohol; they search in coffee shops for people of similar disinclination toward booze.

Men are more likely to find that long stemmed, long haired, faded jeans, no-bra type in coffee houses than on singles cruises. Women seeking a sensitive, esthetic, non-conventional, muscular young man have a better chance of finding him in a coffee house than through computer dating.

Dancing Lessons

Dancing schools hold promise of improving both your dancing and your social life. Although you can also improve your dancing, many dancing schools are unabashedly an expensive way to meet people. Enrollment in some classes is restricted to singles. Beware of disappointment. All male dance instructors are not gigolos. Similarly, very few female dance instructors are call girls.

Who *can* you expect to meet at dance school? As with most commercial places for finding unattached people, females outnumber males. One reason is that unattached females over 35 far outnumber unattached males in that age category. Besides, males still feel more comfortable in taking the initiative and have less need for commercial methods.

Debutante Parties

Upper class people have their own way of paying to meet mates. Debutante "coming-out" parties are a socially acceptable way of purchasing the opportunity to find sex, love, companionship, and fun. The system works, but unless you are very young and wealthy, this method is beyond your reach. Margot, a debutante from Detroit, voices her complaint about coming-out parties:

"I hate those dumb things. My parents wanted me to marry very proper, "Establishment Tom." Forget it. It's like being placed next to somebody while the two of you are still in the incubator. Your mother and father say, 'Don't the two of them make a nice couple? Let's make sure they marry each other at age twenty-one.' You can have that scene. I'll meet a man on my own."

Gay Bars

Gay bars are a singularly effective way for gay males to meet other gay males. Aside from the handful of couples who frequent such bars, most fellows there are looking for action. Similar to straight singles bars, they can be a source of quick sexual encounters or lasting relationships. Sex can be bought or sold in a gay bar. Older gays who are willing to pay for sexual gratification frequent these bars.

Gay bars for females are much less common, and are found mostly in the biggest cities. Almost every medium size town has a male gay bar. Not surprisingly, the name *Dick's* can be a tip-off that the bar is gay.

Bisexual males, looking for a little diversion from heterosexual activity, sometimes visit gay bars. As Perry, a fiftyish clothing store salesman explains it, "I'm lucky, I enjoy it either way. A fellow without sharp teeth or with nice plump hips is about as good as a woman. I take whatever comes along."

Mail-Order Dating

Locating companionship through the mails has already been mentioned in connection with classified advertising. But did you know that entire catalogs of available people can be purchased for a modest fee? One of these entries, appearing in *The Singles Register*, drew 2,000 replies, as reported by the *Washington Post*.

Dynamic redhead, 5 feet 8 inches, 130 pounds, no ties, no strings, loves beach, sailing, surfing, all outdoors, seeks outdoorsman to 35, over six feet, financially secure to share her interests.

Even if the person you meet through a dating magazine has an obvious personality flaw, this can be determined after one or two letters, phone calls, or face-to-face meetings. All you need at any point in time is *one* good relationship. Perhaps it took 2,000 respondents for that "dynamic red-head" to find her prince charming.

Looking at the optimistic side of the picture, here is an ad placed by a somewhat conventional, *normal* but lonely male.

Widower, 5'10", 209 pounds, ordinary app-earance, no children, WASP, but not prejudiced. College graduate pharmacist, non-smoker, light social drinker, quiet type. Enjoy travel, movies, reading and theater. Would like to meet a woman 40 to 50, who is warm and af-fectionate, intelligent and neat, for lasting companionship, sex secondary.

With expectations so realistic, this pharmacist found what he wanted—a decent relationship with an average, middle-aged woman.

Book lovers have a mail order dating service all their own, called Single Book Lovers. Practically everybody who joins SBL is intelligent and look-ing to meet new friends. Chapter 13 presents more information about this very useful service.

Marriage Brokers

Almost indistinguishable from the dating ser-vices described earlier, marriage brokers provide an introduction service. Operators of these firms contend that about ten percent of their clientele find spouses as a result of their services. Your chances of falling into that ten percent vary directly with your attractiveness to other people. The more attractive—physically and psychologically—you are to other people, the more likely it is that a marraige broker will find you a mate. Similar to a banker, the less you need a marriage broker, the more he or she can help you.

Marriage brokers, contends Morton Hunt, cater to the conventional, conservative type of person. The more adventuresome, emancipated (and lucky) people use other methods.

Parents Without Partners

Flora, a 42 year old professional woman, recently divorced, comments about Parents Without Partners:

"What a wonderful way to meet other divorced women about my age. I've belonged to PWP in two towns and it's the same in both places. All I meet are other women in the same predicament. I wish I knew of an organization where I could meet a large number of men. I have more female friends than I want."

PWP is a nation-wide group with over 100,000 members in 1973, and the enrollment continues to swell. Annual membership fees are less than the price of a dinner in a top restaurant. Aside from its social club purpose, PWP provides a variety of activities to help the divorced and separated overcome their unique problems. Activities for children are also provided.

Cindy, a PWP official, notes that nine out of ten PWP members are looking for a mate. Weekly dances are the primary method of introducing males and females. Cindy feels that these dances leave most new women members with an uncomfortable feeling:

"A group of women just stand around hoping

some man will dance with them. Women usually outnumber men two to one, so it's the attractive, younger members who get asked to dance. A lot of women have felt that a bad marriage is better than the humiliation of waiting for a PWP male to ask you to dance."

Female PWP members tend to be healthier than their male counterparts. Most of the male members, it appears, have some serious hang-ups about women, divorce, or responsibility. Some members spend their evenings either in bars or at PWP meetings. Others want to dance with the same woman at every meeting, but never ask her for a real date.

Charlie, a physically attractive, divorced man, has his own peculiar reason for attending PWP meetings:

"Whenever I'm down because of a fight with my girlfriend, I run off to Parents Without Partners. In one night I get enough names to go on a screwing jamboree for three weeks. The women there are very nice and very horny. A guy like me has almost no competition at PWP."

Despite its problems, PWP is an almost foolproof place for a middle-aged male to find a girlfriend or wife. Widowers seeking a return to a stable family situation find PWP particularly valuable. Parents Without Partners is also valuable because it provides solace to those reentering the singles world. Be careful, however, not to get hooked. Some members give up in establishing a social life outside of PWP.

Public Parties and Dances

Would you spend three dollars for an evening of dancing and the prospects of finding an ideal mate? Thousands of unattached people are willing to spend a few dollars for such an adventure. The loneliness industry thus conducts much of its trade at public parties and dances. In New York City alone, on a typical winter weekend, approximately 150 parties and dances open to the public are held. Gatherings of this nature have names like "Singles Mixer," "Tempo Mixer," "Young Sophisticates," and "Young College Graduates Club."

Although the image of these parties and dances has been upgraded since the sleazy dance halls of the 1930's and 40's, many have a dreary atmosphere. Except for a few married males looking for a quick affair and some curiosity seekers, most people attend after having tried most other approaches to mate finding. They have been unable to find stable companions so far, but they have not given up hope.

What does it feel like to attend a public singles dance or party? Most apparent, except for the handful of mixers where entry is denied people over 25, it seems like a trip into the past. Dance numbers played are usually those traditional numbers popular ten to fifteen years ago. People gathered there, however neatly groomed, are dressed in the fashions of the past. It is not unusual for men to wear starched shirts or women, girdles. They also use out of the past expressions such as "that's a *swell* number," or "don't give me any of that jive." (Of course, you may *be* old fashioned.)

Conversation openers are devastatingly bad. Overheard are: "Do you enjoy dancing?", "Do you come here often?", "Is this your first time here?", or "Haven't I seen . . .", or the saddest one of all: "Would you *mind* dancing with me?" (Take pity on the lowly confident male who uses that opener.

It has probably taken all his courage to ask.)

In spite of their willingness to return month after month to these affairs, many women object to the meat market atmosphere at public dances and parties. Laura explains the feeling:

"Being eyed by so many men makes you feel that you are on display for their benefit. They almost poke at you with their hands to see if you are worth dancing with. It's dehumanizing. It feels like a woman is a piece of meat being inspected by fifty men."

What feelings of discomfort do men have at these places? Rejection is the biggest problem faced by men at public parties and dances. Refusing to dance with a man can be a heavy blow to his pride. Ed has some revealing comments:

"What absolutely pisses me off about those lousy dances is the attitude of the women. Some will flat out refuse to dance with you without even first talking to you. How the hell do they know whether or not you're a nice guy just by looking at you? I may not be tall, dark and handsome, but I'm not repulsive either. The next time a girl refuses to dance with me, I'm going to tell her to screw herself."

Can you find a husband or wife at a public party or dance? Few owners of these affairs attempt to document the marriage potential of these gatherings. Among those that do keep score, is the Bachelor—Bachelorette Club of Syracuse, New York. Over a five year period, one marriage for every two dances has occurred. In other words, on the average, every other time the Bachelor and Bachelorettes gather, one couple who meets there, eventually marries.

Should your version of prince or princess charming be a fortyish, somewhat conventional person, you can find what you are looking for at a public party or dance. Be realistic; the majority of "single again" people neither belong to nor pretend to belong to the youth culture.

Rap Group for Singles

Howie found a lover by following up on this advertisement:

RAP GROUP FOR SINGLES
Come rap with us Friday, September 13, 8 PM, $2 before 8, $3 after. Sunday September 15, 7 PM, $2 before 7, $3 after. Informal, refreshments. 3725 South Wintergreen, 442-9789. Safe area of city.

Twelve girls and eight fellows showed up at the session Howie attended. Most members had never rapped in a public group before, but a comfortable feeling among the people quickly developed. A man-woman team ran the sessions. By 9:30 PM the group was heavily into how lonely and sad it is to be unattached and how hard it is to meet a compatible mate.

Howie and Vivian—another rap session participant—tuned into each other's feelings. Few people can be that fortunate on their first singles rap. However, it's a beneficial experience to meet strangers in a new and stimulating manner.

Rent-A-Date

What happens when you are unattached and you need a respectable looking date in a hurry? In most cities you can actually rent a date or escort. Rent-A-Bird, based in Miami, has a stable of 300 to 400 girls who charge $50 for six hours of companionship. Company policy forbids any touching beyond a handshake or a dance.

The director of another rent-a-girl service notes

that men who are interested in the service are carefully screened. Customers must sign an agreement that they will pay for meals, entertainment, and transportation. No sex is expected. Girls rented have a right to leave immediately if any of the contract provisions are violated.

Older, wealthier women sometimes resort to male escort services. Stipulations about "hands off" are left unmentioned. Many of these male escorts are not opposed to receiving large cash gifts from their customers.

Faced with a social emergency, you might find the rental system satisfactory. But almost any other method in this book holds more promise.

Retirement Communities

Senior citizens also need sex, love, companionship, and fun. Retirement communities can be a good hunting ground for such necessities of life. The reason is obvious. You are placed into daily contact with hundreds of people who are in the right age bracket and life circumstances to meet your demands.

Retirement communities are not unlike singles apartment complexes. Card parties and luncheons are used to facilitate social (which could lead to sexual) intercourse. All factors considered, retirement communities are the best commercial method of meeting people open to senior citizens. If you were 75, don't you think you would have better luck in a retirement village than in a disotheque?

Singles Bars

Singles bars are a terrific place to study unattached people. Many of the good and bad opening lines quoted earlier came from conversations overheard in singles bars. Gradually these bars are becoming an acceptable place for the under thirty crowd to shop for companionship. Drinks at singles bars are slightly more expensive than in cocktail lounges, but that additional drink premium multiplies your chance of finding a mate. Curious for some more details about these bars? Read the next chapter.

Singles Clubs

Would you be interested in joining a group of close to middle age, friendly, unattached people? Any club or group with the name "singles" in it will probably fulfill these requirements. Sometimes called "swingles" or "singletons," these groups bring together a group of people who are still looking for the start of a lasting relationship. After five minutes of conversation with a singles group member, don't be surprised to hear an agonizing analysis of what went wrong with his or her marriage.

Dave, divorced and now living with a girl he loves, describes his experiences as a single's club member in Dayton, Ohio:

"Finally, I got up enough strength to quit. It was good for me right after the divorce. But I couldn't take that depressing stuff anymore. It was like people forever telling you about their operation or some old injury. The fellows wore white sweat socks and the girls had on a pound of makeup. Everybody there figured there was something wrong with everybody else. They should have looked into a mirror."

Embarrassingly, the man or woman you clashed with on a computer date may be introduced to you at the Memorial Day Single's Clambake. In their defense, singles clubs offer a variety of activities beyond the Friday night mixer. Trips to the race track, picnics, and golf outings are not uncommon. Hopefully, through it all, two compatible unattached people will find each other.

Singles Resorts

Ned, a businessman, was preparing to check out of a resort hotel where he attended a trade association meeting. "Come on in," he replied to a knock on the door. In walked a maintenance man with an incisive comment about the upcoming weekend.

"Sorry to bother you, but I've got a lot of work to do. I have to tighten the bolts on all these beds. Our big singles weekend is next. Those singles go like crazy when they're here. If I don't tighten the bolts, we'll have a lot of complaints about beds breaking down."

Sexual relations, however, are but a small reason that thousands of people—mostly from the New York metropolitan area—swarm singles resorts. Hopes of matrimony or some other lasting form of companionship is the gravitational pull they have on unattached people.

What might you expect to find at such resorts? Chapter 9 is all about that pinnacle of the mating trade, the singles resort.

Vacations for Singles

Less garrish, less brash, but considerably more expensive are exotic vacation trips for singles. An atmosphere is created that breaks down communication barriers among unattached people. Romantic locations are selected including Paris, Corsica, Tunisia, and the Ivory Coast. The selling point of such trips is that you might be able to form a meaningful relationship with another human being. An advertising brochure for one of these vacation clubs states in part:

"Here we do not impress each other with our money, our status or our clothes. We impress each other with each other ... A bank president and bank teller, without the usual wall of pinstripe between them, make real contact."

An ideal place to meet the jet setter of your dreams? Perhaps. People taking these trips generally have good jobs, are well educated, and don't convey an impression of desperation. But your chances of encountering the vacation fun and sex seeker are high. Ellie has a revealing lament:

"I thought I finally hit upon the vacation of my dreams. As you know, it's no picnic being a divorced woman with three small children. I borrowed money from my parents to find a husband on one of these exotic trips. Two hours after check-in time, I met a surgical resident from Chicago. We clicked from the start. After the second day we found out we liked to go to meals at the same time. We also liked the same kind of dancing and the same sports. He moved into my room. It was heaven.

By the fourth day he told me he loved me and I believed him. We even discussed, in a kidding way, names for children. Five days after I got back he sent me a letter saying, 'Thanks for everything. It was a great vacation and you were a lot of fun. I'm busy with medicine now, but do look me up if in the future you get to Chicago.' I was stunned."

Chapter 8

THE SINGLES BAR

Few unattached people have never exposed themselves at least once to the frustrations and occasional joys of the singles bar. Running through the mind of every unattached customer at a dating bar—except those hungry for a quick sexual encounter—is the vague hope that his or her ideal mate will emerge out of the crowd. Like slot machine players at gambling casinos, those who play the singles game in dating bars are willing to accept many losing experiences for a handful of victories.

Several magazine stories attribute the origins of the singles bar to the resourcefulness of one Berney Sullivan who upgraded his East Side bar in New York, in the early 1960's. Sullivan hired good-looking bartenders, attracting a clientele of airline stewardesses, secretaries, and female teachers. In turn, these women attracted a crowd of junior executives and professional men. A new social phenomenon for meeting people was born. Bars in the past were universally given rock bottom status as a place to start a serious relationship.

Singles bars—all remarkably similar in terms of the interaction among customers—now exist in every city and in many suburbs. Here is the commercial method where the singles game is most frequently, although not the most effectively, played.

What Are They Like?
Singles bars are, above all, superficial, noisy,

and crowded. Any other description would be untrue. For the thousands of unattached people who enjoy superficial, noisy, and crowded places, singles bars are a paradise. For many others, an evening in a singles bar is a humiliating, uncomfortable experience. As Pam describes her one visit to a popular bar:

"After breaking up with Scott, I was willing to try anything to get back into circulation. One Wednesday, after work, I went to The Sturdy Oak with a girlfriend of mine who went there regularly. What upset me the most was the shallow reasons fellows would use to start a conversation or to keep one going with you. I'm proud of my job as a reading consultant in the city school district, but nobody would listen to what I do. Okay, I don't look like a *Vogue* model, nor am I as voluptuous as a *Penthouse* centerfold, but is that a reason for not even talking to me?

"I'll never go back, but if I did, I would know how to play the game. I would wear the most eye-catching attire I could find. Then I would memorize a bunch of phoney nonsensical conversation topics. It was tough trying to relate to fellows at that immature level after having had a good relationship for over two years."

The physical decor at most singles bars is strikingly good. Many have authentic aged wood, comfortable bar stools, elegant furniture, and well appointed restrooms. Even those with sawdust on the floor have a motif consistent with the sawdust. Bartenders and cocktail waitresses (used only in some bars) are usually physically attractive young people, dressed in a manner that fits the physical decor. Men sometimes work as bartenders in dating bars as a method of meeting an almost endless supply of women.

Singles bars sometimes have mechanical contrivances to help you start conversations with strangers. One such device are telephones located on every table: "Hello, table 23. I'm that freckled-faced fellow with red hair in the blue houndstooth sports jacket, over at table 38. Can I come over and join you?" Another gimmick is the "chuck-a-luck," a small wire basket containing two dice. After a woman orders a drink, her bartender shakes the basket. The cost of her drink is then ten times the number showing on the dice. Should she roll a two, the quick witted, unattached male standing next to her would have a natural opening. "Wow, you really lucked out. A Chivas Regal on the rocks for only 20 cents."

Singles who visit these bars usually travel in doubles, triples, or even quadruplets. Women, even more so than men, typically rely on the emotional supprt of a like-sexed friend to help brave the rigors of an evening at a dating bar. Girls sometimes use their friend as an escape vehicle: "That's kind of you to offer to escort me home, but I'm here with my girlfriend, Mary Elizabeth. We came here together and we agreed to go home together." (Girls are *still* using this line to ward off men.)

Resourcefully, men sometimes use a tandem approach to lure women. One pair of jokers in Chicago claimed some success with the "Italian Count" routine. Ben, for instance, would begin a conversation with a girl noting that he was in fact an Italian count who commuted between Italy and the United States on business. At an appropriate moment he would blot his brow with a silk handkerchief. Karl, his confederate, noting the signal from a bar stool nearby, moved toward Ben and his prospect. "Ben, listen to this. You wouldn't believe it. This chick I was talking to says she saw your castle on her trip to Italy last summer." Credentials like these allegedly led to some interesting sexual encounters for Karl and Ben. Being good friends, they took turns playing count and confederate.

People also travel in groups for reasons other than helping each other ward off or attract strangers. Dating bar customers are often regulars who use the bar as a semi-private party; a central meeting place for friends and acquaintances. Now for a closer look at some of the clientele found in singles bars.

The Curious Clientele

Men who frequent singles bars generally hold managerial and professional jobs. Many are executive trainees, high level clerks, or administrative assistants. Very few are production workers or tradesmen. As for the women, school teachers, a few professionals and many, many secretaries can be found in dating bars. A personnel man commented, "I honestly believe you can find more secretaries in a singles bar than in an employment agency."

More important than the types of jobs they hold, is the type of people they are. Singles bar customers can be classified into five different—but not completely mutually exclusive—types: beautiful people, public cock teasers, sex seekers, mate seekers, and the hard core unattached.

The *beautiful people* frequent singles bars to see and be seen by friends. Strutting about in their finest clothing, they are often impervious to newcomers who fall outside of their clique. The center of attention among them is usually the person (male or female) sporting the most ostentatious new fashion. Second in attention drawing power is the person who publically announces the most exotic vacation plans. A prestige item, such as, "It's definitely Mozambique this spring" is good for at least five admiring comments.

Asked why he spent practically all his Wednesday and Friday nights in the same bar, one of these *beautiful people* replied: "You could say it's our version of a private club. I have lots of friends who expect me to be here. If I don't show up for one or two weeks, my friends ask why I'm out of circulation. I get filled in on what's happening with my friends. Besides, I can make all the connections I need for social life right here if I choose to. But even when I'm going with one girl, I still come here to see my friends. I think this place is more fun than a country club."

Public cock teasers, I don't think, even recognize themselves in action. Regularly they visit dating bars to be admired and to flirt, but never to make a good honest social connection. A tip off to their insincerity and shallowness is the mechanical way in which they accept drinks from a stranger: "Thanks for the drink, I have to get back to my friends now," is one oft repeated parry. A confederate of mine confronted one of these public cock teasers about her "look but don't touch" approach to men in bars. Said she, "I guess you could say it's all one big silly game. I'm just not interested in men right now. It's kind of fun though to see how many men will talk to me in one evening and then offer me a drink. When they ask for my name I say something like 'Cherry Pitts' or 'Olive Drab.' I think I'm being funny, but fellows just seem to get angry."

"Cherry Pitts" may not be interested in men for

her own reasons, but many other public cock teasers are simply much better at teasing than playing. One fiery, sexy-looking girl of this variety was so motionless in bed that a man who seduced her thought she had been poisoned. A few others may be lesbians taking out their hostility toward men by holding out false promises to them.

Sex seekers permeate every singles bar. Among their ranks are married men (and an occasional married woman) seeking some gratification *that night* and a variety of men who want to relate to women on only a sexual level. Charlotte advised me about Terry, one such sex seeker.

"Terrible Terry is a good name for him. He is the raunchiest, horniest man I ever met. A few of us exchanged stories about that unbelievable lunatic. Honestly, he asked one girl to raise her dress in a phone booth so they could have a 'quickie' to see if they were compatible before they started dating. His favorite line after buying a stranger a drink is, 'Look honey, I don't play games. Let me know right now. If you are interested in sex, we can spend some time together. If not, let's not waste each other's time.' I'm surprised the slob hasn't moved on to another bar. Girls who know Terry laugh when they see him coming." (Author's note: I think Charlotte meant *approaching!*)

Mate seekers are in large supply in dating bars, particularly among females. More than one middle-aged person has noted that singles bars are no different than any social mixers of the past. Men visit them expecting to get laid, while women hope to find a husband. After enough unattached girls read this book, maybe they will avoid the error of revealing their matrimonial intentions before the second drink. Said anxious Edie, "Let me know right now if you are really divorced. A single girl simply cannot afford to get mixed up with a married man. He usually goes back to his wife and leaves her to start looking all over again."

Many honest, normal people hope to find "someone" in a singles bar, whether or not it leads to matrimony. Marriage to them is of some significance, but something else is even more intriguing. An investment of a few dollars and one evening's time may provide immediate relief from the gnawing discontent arising from loneliness. Most people under thirty have heard of at least one couple who met each other in a singles bar. "If it happened to them it could happen to me."

The *hard core unattached* are woven into the fabric of the singles bar, even though they are in the minority. As mentioned in earlier chapters, these are the unmatables who try every service the mating trade has to offer. Back from a singles cruise, they return to their favorite singles bar to recount their experiences. Sprinkled into their conversation are descriptions of the relative merits of different places to meet people. "I really think the music is better at The Purple Fox, but the drinks are larger here."

Some of the hard core unattached males have lost confidence in their ability to prearrange a date. A singles bar serves as a sanctuary that provides a night out, but circumvents the challenge of having to ask for a date. Fiftyish Harry expresses it this way, "I like this bar. I don't have to bother calling for a date or calling for a girl at her house. If I meet somebody for a few drinks, or maybe a little something else, that's fine. If not, I can still have a good time."

As you might expect, many of the hard core unattached are defensive about why they frequent singles bars. Asked if she felt a sense of futility in having to return to a dating bar week after week, one dowdy woman replied:

"Absolutely not. I come here for one reason only. I like to dance and here you find good music and good dancers." Asked then why she doesn't find one good dance partner and visit a night club with him, she said angrily: "I told you, I like to dance. The music here is excellent."

Can You Find "Someone" There?

Sexual encounters are relatively easy to come by in a singles bar. Assuming your social appeal exceeds that of a gargoyle, and you are willing to invest many drinks and much time, your chances are quite good of scoring. Females have better opportunities than males in the quick sex department. Almost any woman can find a sex partner in a singles bar. Few women can imagine the shock, delight, and disbelief of a man who finds a sex partner in a bar *without even trying*.

A woman approaching men in bars with the simple opener, "You look pretty good to me. How about a little visit to my place?" should be able to score 90 out of one hundred times. Three men will think she is a hooker and be unwilling to pay; two will already be satiated with sex for the day; two will fear being rolled; three will be male homosexuals not looking for female companionship.

Males crude enough to use the same line can be expected to achieve about the opposite results. Ninety out of one hundred women will laugh or ignore him or use one of these lines: "Why, how was I lucky enough to be selected by you for this honor?" or "Why don't you go ahead and get started without me and I'll join you later." A rare answer will be, "Why not?" Male gamblers among my readers will find some challenge in these odds.

Finding "someone"—a lasting, meaningful relationship—is difficult but far from impossible in a singles bar. First of all, unmarried people you encounter in a dating bar are generally unattached. Most healthy people frequent singles bars until they make a decent connection (quite often, *elsewhere* than in the bar). Not unlike a mental hospital, "graduates" return only out of necessity. Barbara summarizes it well:

"Thank God, now that I've found Al, I will never have to make a return visit to one of those dreadful, nightmarish places. Al and I met there, but once we found each other, we only laughed about our experiences there. How could anybody want to go back? I think I spent about three months of Fridays and some weekday nights making the rounds. Even if I hadn't met Al, I had just about had my fill of all the pawing and nonsensical conversation."

Singles bars are good for meeting people if you are in the right age bracket. Despite all their pitfalls, these places now have an almost favorable image as a place for the under twenty-five set to meet lovers and spouses. Couples now publically admit they met in a singles bar. A few are even proud that they selected each other out of a crowd rather than having to be fixed up through a friend. People sometimes ask newly formed couples, "Did you two meet publically?" (usually referring to dating bars). Thousands of unattached people believe that singles bars are the natural meeting and mating grounds for young adults. "How else can you meet people when you're out of college?" naively ask a countless number of men and women. (Statements like these gave me the inspiration to write a book about meeting people.)

Nobody to my knowledge has accurate information about the number of people who meet *the* man or woman in their lives in a singles bar. A handful of bars circulate stories about their cupid index that after awhile are accepted as truth. For instance, the Carriage Inn in Denver at one time claimed 35 marriages over a four year period among its clientele. Singles bars—as is true of most contrived methods of meeting people—seem to lead to a host of superficial, very short-term relationships.

Bob, a graduate student sociologist, offers a reasonable explanation for the temporary nature of most relationships that begin in a dating bar: "Somehow, it's very difficult to get past the phoniness of the first meeting. My friends all note the same odd situation. You call a girl after meeting her in a bar, and things are never the same as they were in the bar. She seems different. You seem different to her. Maybe it's the hang-up of having met under such false circumstances. I can't think of any romance of mine that started in a bar lasting for more than three weeks."

Some Practical Advice

Singles bars are a recommended place for you to play the singles game if you agree with most of the statements listed next. (Should you disagree with most of them, try one of the impromptu situations or systematic efforts I described earlier in the book!)

1. My gambling instincts are strong. Spending a large amount of time for very few payoffs doesn't upset me.

2. My line of chatter is good and my wardrobe

excellent. As I look in the mirror each morning I can truthfully say, "You are an attractive person."

3. I am between 21 and 29 years old, and at least average in appearance. To back up my age, my outlook on life is youthful.

4. Rejection doesn't bother me (very much). If I try to start a conversation with an opposite-sexed person and I get no response, I shrug it off and move on to the next prospect.

5. My sense of humor is keen, but not so subtle that my witty comments require careful thought to catch. My best jokes and one-liners can be understood over the din of a crowded bar.

6. My real motive for spending time in a singles bar is to get laid. Who I lay is less important than the fact that I *do* get laid.

7. My real motive for spending time in a singles bar is to find a spouse or some kind of permanent relationship; but I am willing to accept getting laid as a consolation prize.

8. Passing away time in a singles bar is one helluva lot more fun than spending time alone.

9. Not having to ask for a date has much appeal. It's a relief from pressure when somebody else (in this case the bar owner) does the arranging for me.

10. I enjoy socializing with junior executives and secretaries.

11. Right now my prospect list is absolutely zero, and I want to at least start looking for some social life within the next few days; maybe even tonight.

Chapter 9

THE SINGLES RESORT

The loneliness business reaches its zenith of crassness at the singles resort. At the largest of these resorts, several thousand people *at one time* pursue sex, love, companionship, and fun. Many resort hotels reserve certain times during the year for the unattached (or attached and looking) crowd. Few attached people would feel comfortable caught in the midst of so many unattached people unabashedly searching for companionship. Few unattached people would pay those prices if the resort were populated with ineligibles.

Unattached people throughout the United States can now find a singles resort in their area. Eventually every major resort, including some of the nationally known ski areas in the West, may feature singles weekends. A growing number of dude ranches reserve a few weekends for dudes who prefer to prospect on horseback (or over a beef barbecue). Singles cruises are, in reality, floating singles resorts.

Resorts for singles began in the Catskills, 100 miles due north of Times Square. The Concord and Grossinger's, two resorts world famous for their convention and family trade, turn their facilities over to the Swinging Singles on a scheduled basis. Someone calculated that on one weekend over 5500 singles, predominantly from metropolitan New York, descended upon these two resorts. Several lesser known, but almost as luxurious resorts, were visited by another 1000 mate seekers that weekend. Loneliness is a big business.

What Goes On There?

"Smile," says Sol to an unhappy-looking middle-aged man sitting beside the pool. "You've found the paradise land for singles. Have a ball, this is your week to swing!" Sol, the social director, wants every guest to have fun. During singles week the hotel management is intent upon every guest leaving the hotel happier and more optimistic than when he or she arrived. Every hotel activity, except for the restrooms and the first aid station, is geared toward guests finding mates or dates.

Athletics top the list of resort attractions. Brochures and advertisements for these famous resort hotels truthfully point to exquisite golf, tennis, swimming, and ice skating facilities. Superbly manicured golf greens and tournament specification tennis courts are a delight to the small number of serious athletes among the guests. Singles resort golfers and tennis players are usually duffers and hackers. Male and female alike, they look awkward and make noise, beyond the bounds of good golf or tennis etiquette. (If you read "The Beautiful Byproduct" chapter carefully you will recognize that if a fellow were good at tennis or golf, he wouldn't have to attend a singles resort to find a date.)

Skiing, except at the western ski resorts, attracts even more novices than does tennis or golf. But at the risk of minor sprains and bruises incurred on the bunny slopes, the prospecting is good. As Lola notes: "At least the men you meet attempting to ski are not 100 pounds overweight and post coronary victims." Tumbling over someone at the foot of the hill, sharing the same group beginners lesson, or having an après ski drink are all conversation opening possibilities.

170

Barry has his personal reasons for choosing skiing as a way of meeting women on a singles weekend. "To tell you the truth, I think the finest part of a woman's body is her ass. You can't tell what a woman's ass is like when she's wearing a dress. But when you're trailing her on the rope tow, and she's bent over wearing those tight ski pants, you can stare right at her rear for five minutes. Then I don't have to waste time talking to women who don't have the feature I really want. In the summer, being a gentleman, I let women climb up ahead of me out of the pool. You get one terrific view that way. Then you know who to try and get something going with."

Single swingers may talk about athletics, but they spend more time dining and drinking than exercising. Catskill resorts offer you more food in one day than the normal person biologically requires in five days. The main dining room at the largest resorts resembles a civic center in size. One waiter at the Concord suggested to the management that they utilize golf skooters to transport older guests from the dining room entrance to their seats.

Initiation rites to the singles weekend typically begin at the Friday dinner dance. Surfacing in the minds of most guests are questions like, "I wonder what I'm going to be stuck with at my table; I hope the maitre d' had enough sense not to put me at a table with a bunch of losers." Invariably, people are *not* satisfied with their table. Prince or princess charming is rarely (if ever) waiting for you at your table. Round robin seating is management's thoughtful approach to help you find "somebody" while dining. Every person sits at a different table at every meal. One gala singles weekend yields six sets of new friends. In one singles week (assuming you were financially and psychologically able) you could make twenty-one sets of new friends. Should you encounter the same person more than once, it makes little difference. After one or two days at a singles resort you have heard the same opening lines from so many people that identities become blurred.

Introductions at the dining table are usually strained. Physically attractive people are sometimes made to feel the most uncomfortable, being subjected to questions like: "Who would have thought a pretty girl like you would be at a singles weekend?" or "Don't good looking fellows like yourself have girls falling all over them at home?"

"Where are you from" often precedes, "What do you do?" A secretary from Providence, Rhode Island refused to return to a Catskill resort because mention of Rhode Island stamped her a GUD (geographically undesirable). "I even met a creep from New York who didn't have a driver's license. He said he didn't need one because he made it a policy never to date *out-of-towners*."

Cocktail parties (provided by the management) are an extension of the dining approach to lining up some social prospects. People flit about, often adorning name tags, greeting other singles. Nobody has to make the pretense that they have attended the party for reasons other than improving their social life. In contrast, if two swingers meet at the tennis courts, both can proclaim a primary interest in tennis.

Unfortunately for female egos, males feel under no obligation to use sensitivity and tact upon introduction. "I'm Mike from the City and I'm looking for a good time. Are you interested?" is an oft-repeated opener. Women themselves feel

172

under no obligation to be coy in searching for information: "Are you or are you not married?" is an oft-repeated question.

Hors d'oeuvre crashers (or resort parasites) worm their way into most of the big parties. Here is how it works: David, an impecunious Wall Street employee, heads for the Catskills for the weekend. He rents a room in a cheap motel located near the posh resorts. Dressed in his best suit, he slithers his way into the resort of his choice during cocktail hour. (Typically, he has sent for a travel brochure beforehand to apprise him of the weekend schedule.) Should Dave line up a good prospect, he asks to meet her after dinner *outside* the dining room. Maitre d's make life difficult for men like David; they require identification before seating a guest.

Even if David, or his counterparts, do not score with a woman, they have treated themselves to an hors d'oeuvre dinner and some punch bowl cocktails. Aside from the immorality of stealing food from the owners, isn't a person like David really carrying out a harmless prank? "Hell, no," says Ina. "I save my money to come to a resort hoping to find a man with some money. If a guy is too poor to pay for a stay at a resort, I have no interest in spending time with him."

Games for adults are another item in the people meeting smorgasbord offered by resort hotels. Simple Simon has an adult version. "Simon says everybody who wants to meet somebody should raise their hand." "Simon says everybody who is single should raise their right shoulder." "Simon says everybody who is a virgin should raise their right leg." Hundreds laugh while a few less thick-skinned people grimace to combat nausea in response to Simon Says.

According to one social director, Simple Simon is one of the best ice-breakers. "People who come up here are a little stiff and afraid. A few minutes of Simple Simon and they realize everybody else here has the same problem. I wouldn't be surprised if some of our best romances began right in the middle of Simon Says."

Computer dating and get-acquainted parties are used in almost game-like fashion at the singles resort. "Are you on my list" is the canned opener available to anybody who enrolls in computer dating for the Singles Week. Carole, a young nurse who works in a home for the aged, used a pleasant variation of this line: "Hi, Mr. Stranger. Even if you aren't on my list, you and I could be compatible. Did you know that computers sometimes fail to match up the very people who should be matched up?"

Social directors cannot be faulted for lack of creativity in dreaming up new games for adults. A flyer from the world's largest resort describes an interesting event taking place at a singles Irish Weekend (to a clientele 99.8 percent non-Irish):

CO-ED SPLASH & SAUNA PARTY ... As our Italian friends would say, "Let's splash 'til the sauna comes up!" One word of caution, please don't drink the water. It may look like water to you (actually, it's Irish whiskey colored blue!) ... which accounts for the many happy, glowing swimmers ...

Self-development can improve your social life, even at a singles resort. Among such mind-improving activities are duplicate bridge tournaments and lessons, lectures about child rearing, and stock market forums. As explained by Laura, "At least there is hope at these things. The men who attend have some sense and are willing to take a few minutes from eating food and chasing women to learn something worthwhile. Women who drop into the educational events also seem healthier than those who hang out at the pool or bar all day. A divorced friend of mine actually met her new husband at a lecture on how divorced fathers should act with their children."

"Hanging out" or making casual appearances is considered by some as the best method of making contact at a singles resort. Nobody needs to apologize to anybody for making a casual, "Just happened to be standing here" contact. Non-athletes get considerable mileage out of the cocktail-in-the-hand sports-attire approach. The cocktail allows easy access to the opener, "Won't you join me for a drink?"

An outstanding feature of the hanging-out routine is its flexibility and versatility. Should you play volley ball, bingo, or duplicate bridge you have committed yourself to a block of valuable time. Few people—even at a singles resort—are boorish enough to walk away from a duplicate bridge or volley ball game because no good prospects are also playing. The casual routine of simply standing around allows you to meander from location to location in your pursuit of friendship.

Singles resorts, from a logistical standpoint, are better suited for group than one-to-one sex. Guest rooms are typically packed with two, three, or four like-sexed people. The clientele at singles resorts, however, are distinctly too old fashioned for group sex. Guests are then faced with the dual problem of with whom and *where* to experience sex. Ingenious solutions to the latter problem have been found.

According to singles resort legend, the person who finds a willing partner uses an elementary signal system to his or her roommate(s). A piece of masking tape on the door, a "please do not disturb" sign, a prophylactic wrapper under the doormat, or a "there was an anonymous phone call for you" note are some of the agreed upon signals to insure sexual privacy.

Seasons, of course, exert an influence on where sex is practiced at a singles resort. Golf courses at night—well-manicured putting greens in particular—are considered quite adequate except for those troublesome chlorphyll stains. Adults who haven't experienced the contortions of automobile sex in twenty years are often reawakened to such pleasures at a singles resort. Linen closets, although usually locked, are exceptional hideaways for vertical sex. Fire escapes are passable, providing you bring an air mattress or its equivalent.

Lynn, a thirty-fivish school teacher put her class room experience to good use at a singles resort. Leon and she met poolside on the first night of the big Singles Week. Both encumbered by three roommates, she bribed the day care counselor to lend her the nursery school key. Leon and Lynn then had their private tryst. According to my informant, neither felt guilty about having sex with pictures of Mother Goose and Humpty-Dumpty as a backdrop.

Who Do You Meet There?

Experienced players of the singles game will find few surprises at a singles resort. Many of the characters in that drama have already made their appearances at cruises, social clubs, and matchmaking bureaus. Unlike places such as Parents Without Partners, the management feels under pressure to balance the male-female ratio. Be prepared to encounter a variety of interesting people ranging from the mid-twenties to a few pre-retirement swingers. Marty, Pauline, and Richard are typical of the people you will meet at a singles resort.

Marty, a 41 year old bachelor from Boston, is handsome, debonnaire, witty, and neurotic. A regular at singles weekends, Marty attracts large crowds of women, generally for conversation only. Each time another woman says, "Marty, how come a handsome looking man like you isn't married," Marty beams in appreciation. Adorned with a pinky ring and a $250 suit, he impresses many women. Early in a conversation with a stranger, Marty makes reference to his boat and portfolio of stocks. Enid, a social worker, has Marty pegged:

"This fellow is what you would call a narcissistic character. He really loves himself. He gets his big kicks in life from women fawning over him. If somebody doesn't mention that he's good looking, he moves on to somebody else. Despite the fact that he must have been seen with fifty women during the singles week I was there, I don't think any one contact was anything but superficial. I don't have enough evidence to be sure, but I think the only person who can excite Marty is Marty."

Pauline, a 36 year old office supervisor, is the divorced mother of three children. Formerly married to a surgeon, Pauline is under constant pressure from her mother to remarry. Having read a magazine article about a singles resort, Pauline's mother presented her with enough money to cover the cost of one week at the Concord. "It's the least I can do for my darling daughter who has had so much misfortune in her life." To round out this generous offer, the mother agreed to stay with Pauline's children for the week.

At the resort, Pauline displayed all the signs of

a person who has never entangled herself emotionally from her former marriage. The thread of her opening conversation with prospects is a tip-off that Pauline is still reliving her marriage. Here is what she told Jack, a middle-aged man who bought her a martini:

"Pleased to meet you. I'm Pauline Gordon. I'm from the city. Maybe you've heard of my ex, Dr. Max Gordon, a very well-known surgeon and handsome as the devil. Max and I were divorced eight years ago. He's married and he seems to be very happy. He married a girl twenty years younger than himself. My children say she is more like a sister than a mother to them. What do you think of a man who marries a girl that young? Do you think he's trying to prove something to himself?

"I work as a supervisor in an office. Do you know that I work forty-five and fifty hours every week and also try to be a good mother? Max is probably sitting beside his pool with his young chick of a wife while I'm mowing the lawn outside the little house he left us. How much alimony do you think a wealthy doctor should pay? I'm sorry. What did you say your name is? What is your ex-wife like?"

Richard, a 31 year old computer scientist, found a haven in the Singles Week. Timid and shy, Richard has a difficult time picking up girls. Slender in build and average in appearance, Richard's primary asset at a singles resort is that he is a living, breathing, unattached and sincere male. In addition, he has a good paying job. Richard has found one good romance on each of his three trips to a singles resort. Realistic Richard explains:

"As you might guess, I am not the Don Juan type. My thing is computers, not chasing women. I don't think it's a good policy to date women from the office. I heard of one manager who ended the virginity of a twenty-five year old computer programmer and she bugged him for a year, even asking for a bigger raise. He was afraid she would tell his wife. Bars aren't good for a person with any sense, so what do you have left? You could say I'm too old to be fixed up.

"At a resort, you don't have to keep on hustling and getting rejected. I especially like the older women. Some aren't glamour girls and they wear too much make-up, but at least they are appreciative. If you just stand there with a drink in your hand, a nice woman will start talking to you. Besides, many are intelligent people with interesting jobs. I despise talking to dumb women.

"My plans now are to find a wife at one of these resorts. Each time I vacation there, I get about four good leads for dates in the city. I figure that for a total investment of a couple of thousand dollars, I should be able to find a satisfactory wife. I don't feel like starting a new family, so one of those under thirty-five divorced women with children might not be too bad for me."

How Well Does It Work?

Are you looking to get laid in a hurry, or are you trying to line up a long term romance? Singles resorts are set up more for mate finding than for instant sex. (Forget what the maintenance man in Chapter 7 said about resorts; he's no expert.) Finding a partner for sex, as I mentioned earlier, is sometimes easier than finding a *place*. The "swinging singles" crowd often cuts down on expenses by sharing rooms. Patience helps. Sex-seekers should use the resort to line up a number of prospects for later use. Be prepared for the inevitable post-resort letdown when you phone. "Your name sounds familiar, but I met so many men that week, I'm not sure which one you were. I talked to about five Dave or Davids. Which one were you?"

Resort owners make extravagant claims about their cupid index. One social director modestly claims that thousands of marriages began during his Simple Simon games. Management of another well known resort claims enough marriages to equal the population of a small city. More important than how many people find each other at these resorts, is *who* finds each other.

Singles resorts are a gathering place for those close to middle age, many of whom are seeking long term involvements. Older people, with surprising frequency, find mates at the singles resorts. Senior citizens or those approaching such status in life are brutally realistic in their demands. "She has an air-conditioned mobile home; I have a good car and a good pension. We both like gin rummy. Why not? Who wants to be alone?"

Some Practical Advice

1. Singles resorts are best used as a source of potential dates for future use. Unless a fantastic romance falls in your lap, avoid devoting your entire singles weekend or week to one person. Marriages generally stem from relationships that gained momentum after a few dates back home.

2. Discount by twenty-five percent most of the fanciful things people at the resort tell you about themselves. Many "stewardesses" or "models" turn out to be file clerks and many "executives" turn out to be assistant managers. Incomes are lower and ages are higher when reality hits. Back in the city, should you and that resort romance get together, you might want to verify a good many interesting facts about your new friend.

3. Spend the few extra dollars to get a private or semi-private room if you expect to have sexual relations in privacy. Few of the people you will meet at a singles resort will feel comfortable having sex while your roommate(s) watch.

4. Resist using the hackneyed opener, "This is my first time at this type of thing. Have you been here before?" About one-third of all resort guests use this line. Be unique.

5. Beware of the extremely good-looking male or female at these resorts. Usually they are harboring some personality problem that prevents them from forming sound relationships with an opposite-sexed person. At least be alert to this possibility to avoid a crushing disappointment later.

6. If you intend to contact a person you meet at a resort later, make sure she (or he) is able to remember you. Have a long, somewhat unique conversation or better yet, have a third person snap a picture of you two. Send it to your prospect before making your phone call.

7. Astound, amaze, and bedazzle people at a singles resort by being honest. Simply and straightforwardly tell them who you are and why you are there. Try this one, "I'm Larry Baxter, an accountant. I came here to meet some women because I'm unattached."

Chapter 10

THE SINGLES VILLAGE

Your stay at a singles resort can be permanent if you move to a singles apartment complex. Hundreds of thousands of unmarried—and a handful of married—people pay a small rental premium to live in these country-club style arrangements. Every weekday night, and all day Saturday and Sunday, the singles village management structures some activity to facilitate your finding sex, love, companionship and fun. From mixed doubles tennis tournaments to champagne brunches, there is some organized activity to help you make a social connection.

The idea of attracting tenants by offering extraordinary opportunities for meeting opposite-sexed people began—as you might suspect—in southern California. Similar adults-only housing complexes then sprung up in other warm, sunny climates as land developers elsewhere envied the success of the California experience. Now, singles complexes are found in locations such as Washington, D.C. and Long Island, despite their more seasonal climate.

Recently, the original developers of the singles village have pointed their investment dollars in other directions, but the boom is still at least a semi-boom. Many singles-only apartments now request young adults without children ("young" meaning anybody not yet retired). A few phone calls to apartment realtors will help you locate the nearest Disney World for the unattached. As a secondary source of information, consult a few airline stewardesses. Legend has it that stewardesses are the first to learn about and inhabit apartment complexes for singles.

The Village Way of Life

What better way to describe what life is like in a singles village than to give you a blow-by-blow (no pun intended) description of one week in the life of a "typical" resident. Bruce, a 36 year old manager in an insurance company, is divorced and has been living at Birchwood Garden Apartments for eleven months. Currently on the loose because the girl he had been dating for three months couldn't cope with the size of his alimony payments, Bruce is eager to rebuild his social life.

Home Monday at five, Bruce heads for one of the three pools at Birchwood. Five minutes after setting up his beach chair, a bronzed muscular man about twenty-five urges Bruce to join in a co-ed volleyball game that has started up outside the pool area. "Sorry, I'm not in the mood today; things are very heavy." Bruce reasons that women hunting is never good for him during a game of volleyball, because most of the women players are looking for younger men.

After a quick dip in the pool, Bruce makes his first contact: Bev, a spectacular-looking 45 year old music teacher, asks if she might sit next to him. Bruce responds enthusiastically to Bev's invitation to stop by for a drink at his convenience, offered after ten minutes of conversation. While having a martini before his frozen beef pie dinner, Bruce reasons, "I have to get started rebuilding my social life somewhere. Why not Bev?" After a brief phone conversation, Bev and Bruce agree to meet at her apartment at 9:30.

In the interim, Bruce takes out a yellow pad and labels the top sheet of paper, "Source of Supply."

Bev is first on his list; he has one hour to further develop his list before their date. Bruce then takes off to the jogging track for a quick look at some prospects. He explains why: "Jogging has its unique advantage for finding women. I like girls with nice firm breasts. It's the thing around here to jog in a sweatshirt without a bra. You can tell in just a few strides if a girl is firm or floppy." By the second run around the track, Bruce has one lukewarm prospect, Anne. She responds in a puff, "O.K. so you want to make contact. I'm Anne Cobb, listed under 'A.L. Cobb.' If you really want, give me a call; but I'm kind of busy."

Bruce and Bev find out by one A.M. that they are physically compatible, giving Bruce the feeling that Birchwood is well worth the rent. In less than thirty minutes of looking, Bruce had lined up his bed partner—not a record for a singles complex, but still a respectable showing. After leaving Bev's place at six-thirty A.M., Bruce decides to wait until that night to add to his supply of prospects.

Courtesy of Birchwood's management and coordinated by the activities director, Tuesday night is the "Ides of March" hamburger and chicken roast. Name tags, in the shape of hearts, are used to help newcomers get acquainted. Bruce thrusts his attention on Gwendolyn, a carefully coiffured blonde. "Hello, I'm Bruce Carlton from Security Mutual Insurance Company." Replies Gwendolyn, "Get lost, Brucey, baby. I moved in here with my boyfriend and, besides, I despise insurance salesmen."

By nine P.M. Bruce has experienced three other unprofitable attempts at contact. Back at his apartment, he decides to call Bev, reasoning, "An older gal is always lonely. Spending the night with her should be a sure thing." Bev is home, but has some disheartening news for Bruce. "I don't think it would be a good idea for me to see you anymore. My boyfriend and I had lunch today and I think he's serious about me again." Discouraged, Bruce retreats to El Club, Birchwood's singles bar, open only to members. (Renting an apartment there automatically grants you membership.)

El Club is busy for a Tuesday. Several people are still talking about the Valentine's Day extravaganza. Central to the discussion is whether the party lasted twenty-four or thirty-six hours. Dick Mason, an aerospace engineer, volunteers the juiciest tidbit of the evening: "One of my buddies tried to seduce that singer with the sexy voice and she turned out to be a female impersonator. You can imagine how my buddy felt when he reached down into the singer's pants. Instead of a warm pussy he felt a hot cock."

Later Bruce escorts a girl named Cindy—an attractive special education teacher—back to her apartment. After an unsuccessful attempt at seduction, Bruce is told, "Here's how it is. If you call I will probably go out with you. But I never go to bed with anybody from Birchwood. No matter what line you give me, I know that if we have sex tonight, tomorrow you'll be describing it to your friends at the pool or back at El Club."

Wednesday night Bruce heads for the Drama Encounter, an amateur theatre group that stages shows and conducts impromptu script readings. Realizing that El Club can become discouraging, Bruce welcomes the opportunity to pursue women in an intellectual setting. He volunteers to read some lines from an Arthur Miller play. Valli, his co-reader, is a six-foot-one Indian girl. Bruce eagerly writes down Valli's number after hearing a poem she whispers in his ear between acts:

> *Later you and I can speak;*
> *You'll find me quite Greek.*
> *Any orifice you wish,*
> *I think is deelish!*

Bruce consults "The Crier," the Birchwood activities flyer to select a locale for Thursday night's prospecting. Volley ball, beginning at 8:00, is the fun way to meet people, suggests the activities director for that night. As the flyer states, "There is always room for one more."

Janice, a speech therapist, is the productive yield from one and one half hours of volley ball. Reasoning that a speech therapist is closer to a nun than a nymphomaniac in sexual attitudes, Bruce wisely asks for her number without pushing his luck further for that evening. Before parting, Janice mentions, "It's nice to meet a mature person for a change. I hope to see you around the pool sometime. I'll be away for the weekend."

Buoyed up emotionally because of Janice, Bruce heads with confidence to El Club Friday night. Six drinks later, Bruce finds the bar scene more depressing than exhilarating. Three girls tell Bruce that they mostly date men who are part of their regular crowd. Two divorced women seem more intent upon reopening old emotional wounds than upon looking positively at life. One airline stewardess insists on babbling away about air travel, and shows no interest in learning about Bruce. Finally, one girl, who Bruce finds intriguing, tells him that she is visiting the club simply because her boyfriend is out-of-town.

Convinced now that meeting women at Birchwood is done best outside El Club, Bruce stays in motion Saturday. Dressed in carefully faded sports attire, he does his wash, waxes his car, and spends two hours at the tennis area. During a group tennis lesson—courtesy of the management—Bruce makes another contact. Elaine is a frail, tall girl with surprisingly plump buttocks showing through the edges of her tennis panties. Her opener is, "You don't even need these lessons; you're so good at tennis." Bruce returns her serve with, "Let's you and I hit a few after the lesson."

Again feeling the wonders of this singles paradise, Bruce invites Elaine to that evening's Las Vegas Night. Back at his apartment Elaine shows promise of passion but wards off Bruce's advances with the curt comment, "Come now, Bruce. You don't believe all those lurid stories that have appeared in magazines about Birchwood. I'm hardly the sexually liberated type. I think sex is terrific—between two married people."

Sunday morning is the champagne brunch where all the "in" people of Birchwood gather. By Sunday there are few surprises left for Bruce. Four different men say, "War is hell," when some other male is quicker on the draw in lighting a woman's cigarette. At least three different groups are laughing about the latest fable circulating at Birchwood. "An older gal moved in who was really on the make. She made a mistake one night that cramped her style. Somehow she confused her tube of polident with foam spermicide. She had to call maintenance to help pry loose a fellow she met that night at El Club."

Who Lives There?

Birchwood, or any other singles complex, is only as exciting (or dull) as its inhabitants. Bruce Carlton's week of experiences at Birchwood has given you one glimpse at the cast of characters you might encounter at a singles village. Jack, Hope, and Carole are a representative slice of other residents.

Jack, a 27 year old space salesman for a newspaper, has lived in a singles village for two years —longer than most tenants. Jack sees himself as a playboy, a man of the times, a fun lover, and a good sport. Asked what he enjoys best about life at his complex, Jack replied, "The turnover of chicks. You wouldn't believe all the new talent that moves in and out of here every month. Some chicks get married and move away, some get turned off by the fast pace of living. But there is still a waiting list of new gals to take their place. During the summer a lot of school teachers move in with their friends who live here year-round. Can you imagine adding a couple of hundred possibilities over a three month period? You would have to be crazy to take a vacation away from this spot."

Jack requires a large supply of women. Never has he had a romance last beyond three months; and even that relationship was on the decline after six weeks. Despite Jack's preference for short term relationships with women, he is well liked. His apartment is the envy of many other villagers. Although furnished by management, Jack has added a small museum of interesting prints and maintains a wine rack, acceptable to the most discriminating enologist.

Jack can be best understood by revealing his most treasured possession. Kept inside his apartment safe is a small black address book (Jack doesn't claim to be original) containing a list of over one hundred names. Following each name is a coded number; "1" indicates intercourse on the first date; "2" indicates intercourse by the second date; "3" by the third date, and so forth; "N" indicates she was *not interested*.

Hope, a 24 year old kindergarten teacher, moved to her singles promised land from Portland, Oregon. Known by some friends as "Goodie Two Shoes," or "Little Miss Hymen," Hope is a strawberry blonde with sun freckles. Shortly after moving in, Hope joined two different committees to improve the quality of living in her singles village. One committee attempted to set up a bottle and tin can recycling center at Birchwood. Committee number two planned to bring senior citizens and inner city children to the complex on weekends, so they too could enjoy the benefits of country club living. Although supporters for her causes were in scant supply, Hope won the respect of many for her ability to work hard and keep smiling.

Hope explains what she enjoys best about life in the complex: "I have just never met so many wonderful people before. We're just one big bunch of kids having a ball. I just love the parties given here. You can find a party somewhere every night. You don't even have to be invited. It's sort of an unwritten rule. If you hear a party going on, you just knock on the door and enter. Everybody is informal around here. Nobody is a stuffed shirt. You're always meeting some nice new friends this way.

"Another terrific thing about this place is that you can have fun without being serious with a fellow. Without those parties with so many people in the room, a lot of fellows might want to be alone with you in their apartments. This way you're always in a crowd so nothing too heavy can develop. You could say that living here is a very safe thing for a single girl to do. In fact, now that I bring it up, I think the reason I like it here so much is that it's just like living in a big college dormitory!"

Carole, a 31 year old personnel officer in a

bank, has moved to Twin Oaks (a well-appointed singles complex) with a specific plan in mind. Carole has been hurt in a relationship with John, a separated man she had been dating for five years. John called her at her office one day with an urgent sounding request. "Carole, I have some important information for you. Let's have dinner tonight." Expecting to learn that John and his wife had finally agreed to initiate divorce proceedings, Carole was shocked by John's "information."

"That wretched human being; he told me coldly that he and his wife had agreed to get back together again. In one moment of agony, all the admonitions friends had given me about dating married men made sense. I loved him. I gave him five crucial years of my life. He told me that we should get together for lunch from time to time providing we didn't make it too obvious. I could have hit him with the wine bottle. He made me feel like scum, dirt, filth, an unwanted woman. Okay, so now I'm here at Twin Oaks picking up the pieces and rebuilding my life."

Carole is indeed rebuilding her social life, but with a planfulness that could only come from a background in business. She has put together some rigid guidelines for extending a relationship with a man even beyond one date. He has to be single, under 32, in apparent good physical health, and hold a managerial or professional job. Asked, "Why so rigid?" Carole replied:

"I'll never get taken again. Now that I've made my break, I want the best. I want a man who is about my age or younger so I can have a vigorous man around the house until I'm too old to enjoy him. If you marry a man about twenty years older than yourself, later on in life you wind up becoming his nurse and housekeeper. From what I've read, my sexual peak is still in the future. A man about my age is already heading downhill sexually, but I know it's tough to find a man ten years younger than myself who fits my other requirements.

"I expect a man with a high-status job because I think I have high status. Not many women are bank officers at my age. I'm also well educated, intelligent, and friends say that I'm considered attractive.

"To make sure that a man is in fact single and in good financial shape, I do the same thing we would do at the bank about a person who wanted to borrow a large sum of money. I run a Retail Credit Check on him. If his story doesn't groove with their story, I drop him right away. Never again will I be stung."

A True Sexual Paradise?

The management at one of the poshest singles apartment complexes now has a policy of refusing to grant interviews to outsiders unless they present appropriate credentials. Interviews granted in the past, according to the management, led to exaggerated and untrue stories. In truth, for many people life in a singles complex *is* a sexual paradise and for many others life there is a sexual desert. Not surprisingly, the people—male and female—who find a sexual paradise in the singles village, probably were no strangers to paradise before they arrived. Similarly, those who find a desert there, never found an oasis in the world outside.

"Sex as Athletics in the Singles Complex," the fun title of a recent *Saturday Review of Society* article, features the escapades of one Charley Hazzard, a finder of sexual paradise. Charley, a divorced man about 36, accomplished the Olympian feat of bedding down 79 women in one year at Woodway Square Apartments in Houston, Texas. Gentlemanly rules for the contest prevailed: ". . . each contestant was expected to keep an honest score on himself and share the names, telephone numbers, and sexual preferences of the women who added to his total."

Similar tales can be told. Mickey, a muscular yet esthetic-looking construction worker at Twin Oaks, dated only girls on the pill. Mickey's logic for doing so was opportunistic but impeccable: "It worked this way. I keep a master calendar of the cycles of about six women I'm dating. This way I know who is having a period and at what time. In five months I have not had to spend the night with a woman having a period. Before the pill you just couldn't operate this way. Periods are unpredictable as hell if a chick isn't on the pill."

Penelope, a well known figure at Twin Oaks, creates a sexual paradise for herself and selected friends that can best be described in verse:

"Oral, anal, genital, whatever your pleasure.
Date me, and find your treasure.
I squirm, I nip, I lick, I screw.
Have it one on one, or two with two.

Girls like Penelope, much to the chagrin of many men who newly arrive at a singles village, are in the small minority. Villagers with the luck or talent of Charley Hazzard or Mickey are also in the minority. A crushing disappointment to many male newcomers to singles apartment complexes is that girls, just like anywhere else, usually reserve sexual relations for men they are dating regularly. Rarely, if ever, is a new male member to the village greeted by a swarm of females who shout en masse, "We want your body." As one golf pro crudely describes the sex scene at his singles complex, "You still have to be nice to girls to get laid, and even nicer to get blown!"

What about the mate-finding possibilities at the singles village? Whatever evidence we have suggests that you are more likely to find a sexual than a marital paradise. In some complexes, males outnumber females; in others, the reverse ratio is true. In either situation most of the male villagers did not sign a lease in order to find a wife. Sex, love, companionship and fun—without the constraints imposed by marriage—is typically their goal. Obviously many people *do* find their mates at a singles complex, just as many people *do* find their mates at singles bars. An observation by Gerry, a young veterinarian, is illuminating: "I get the impression that most people who leave this place because they marry, marry somebody they met *outside* the complex. Some people think of this place as a social playground. Serious relationships are confined to the outside world."

Some Practical Advice

Give serious thought to relocating to a singles apartment complex—even for awhile—if most of the following statements accurately express your feelings:

1. An exciting country club life style is for me, although my neighbors would have furniture, drapes, carpeting, and dishes identical to mine.

2. I want to save on gas by doing my prospecting within walking distance.

3. I have no children, or my children live with somebody else.

4. I enjoy brash, fun-loving, party-going people and I want to live surrounded by them.

5. I dislike solitude and privacy.

6. My athletic tendencies favor an environment with regulation tennis courts, an olympic-size swimming pool, Jacuzzi whirlpool baths, basketball, ping pong, volley ball, and shuffleboard (for when I'm tired).

7. It's important to me to share conversation with strangers about parties, who is dating whom, and my sexual conquests (real or imagined).

8. I favor a combination of healthy outdoor and indoor entertainment.

9. I'm looking for a younger group of people who, similar to me, want to carve out a carefree lifestyle for themselves.

Chapter 11

MATCHMAKING BY COMPUTER

Sex, love, companionship, and fun can only be yours if you find another person to date. Furthermore, these experiences will only be temporary unless you and the person you find are compatible. Computer dating services have been in operation since the late 1960's to help people find compatible mates. Almost everybody has heard about computer dating, but fewer people understand what is actually involved when you commit yourself to finding other people by this method.

How Does It Work?

Underlying computer dating is a simple principle. A compatible mate for you would be one that shows the same patterns of likes and dislikes as you. Hypothetically, let us assume that Max only cares about two things in a female. First, that she is between five feet three and five feet nine in height; second, that she is a college graduate. Max—again very hypothetically—would have an easy time of mate selection. Any female college graduate of medium height would turn him on. Hundreds of other possible things about people, such as age, occupation, sexual proclivities, dentures versus no dentures, hair color, weight, physical attractiveness, political attitudes, and so forth, are important to most of us in choosing a mate.

What computer dating offers people who are trying to upgrade their social lives is a chance to meet people with whom you are compatible with in about fifty areas. Correspondingly, you are asked to complete a lengthy questionnaire which is supposed to accurately reveal your unique pattern of preferences. Electronic computers are then called upon to perform the almost astronomical task of finding a handful of other-sexed people with a profile similar to yours. If the job were done with scientific precision, literally millions of comparisons would be made before finding even one "compatible" for you. Next are samples of the type of questions that appear on computer dating forms. (Basic factual information about a person, such as age, phone number, and marital status, of course, is always obtained.)

My feelings on sex before marriage are:
    Strongly in favor of——
    In favor of——
    Neutral——.
    Against——
    Strongly against——

Are you:
    Very shy——
    Shy——
    Slightly shy——
    Average——
    Slightly outgoing——
    Very outgoing——

People whose opinions and attitudes differ from mine:
    Are in need of more knowledge——
    Are entitled to their own point of view——
    Simply have a different background than I have——

I enjoy making big decisions: True——
                                 False——

My interest in marriage is:
    Very strong——
    Strong——

Moderate——
Weak——
Very weak——
My date should be:
Protestant——
Catholic——
Jewish——
Not associated with a religious group——
Any religion——
A woman's place is in the home, not out trying to compete with men.   True——
False——
Your fiancee informs you that she has had relations with another man. You would probably:
Break the engagement——
Tell her that if she does it once more, the engagement is off——
Tell her about your own romantic activities——
Feel that sharing this secret with you will strengthen your relationship——
Tell her that it is of no consequence——
You have taken a new girlfriend out to dinner five times. When you ask her to cook dinner for you, she claims she doesn't know how to cook. You would probably feel:
Angry——
Rejected——
Delighted——
Indifferent——
Manipulated——
Which of the following would you prefer:
Loving a man who did not love you——
Being loved by a man you did not love——
Neither loving nor being loved unless the feeling was mutual——
How important is it that your date own an automobile?

Very important—— .
Moderately important——
Unimportant, he can borrow mine on dates—

After you have paid the fee and mailed back the completed questionnaire, the computer dating service attempts to match you up with a group of compatibles. The more elaborate (and expensive) computer matchmaking outfits conduct interviews with all applicants and also screen them for criminal records, marital status and other significant information. Then you are sent biographical sketches about each person on your list. Less expensive programs simply provide you with a list of names, addresses, and phone numbers. Arriving in your mail box might be a decorated sheet of paper with an intriguing message:

Dear Member:

Here are the people that our computer has scientifically selected for you. Each person on your list has interests and feelings very similar to your own, and THEY WANT TO MEET YOU! Don't forget, you have been selected for them, too. They have your phone number and might be thinking of calling you. Take the initiative. Call them first. After all, each person on your list is very similar to you in likes and dislikes. Don't miss out on a great opportunity. Call now and meet perhaps your perfect mate.

Can It Find You A Mate?

Before generalizing about whether or not computer dating can assist you in finding a meaningful relationship, let us look at two case histories: one heartening and one discouraging.

Sandra Bernstein, age 35, is a Hunter College graduate. The head librarian at a Brooklyn branch of the public library, she lived with her mother in a small apartment. Married at age 29, after many years of searching for a suitable mate, her husband died one year later in an automobile accident outside of JFK airport. Six years later, Sandra was still searching for another mate. She had tried the popular methods of mate finding such as referral through friends, social clubs, and four different singles weekends at the Concord Hotel. After reaching 35, Sandra's concerns about being alone intensified. Sitting home one Saturday night, she filled out an application for Find-A-Mate, a $250 computerized date referral service.

Alan Boswell, a 48 year old widowed lawyer, with four children, joined Find-A-Mate about the same time. Sandra and Alan were put on each other's list. Alan called Sandra one Wednesday, inviting her to his house in Forest Hills for dinner that Sunday. He explained that on Sundays, he and his children have a family cook-out in their backyard, and that this would be a good way to get to know each other. Sandra, after thinking over the situation, agreed that this would be a unique and healthy way to get acquainted. Everybody immediately got along with everybody. Alan thought Sandra was delightful. He always enjoyed frail, conservative-looking women. Sandra thought Alan was manly, responsible, mature, and compassionate and did not find his modest height and portly physique unattractive. The four children liked Sandra for different reasons. Marty thought she was good at story telling. Carol liked the way she didn't monopolize her father's time. Alex said she was a good sport. Barbara, the oldest, thought Sandra was warm and understanding.

After five months of enjoying a variety of activities together as a family unit, Alan and Sandra were married. One afternoon, about seven months after their wedding date, Sandra was listening to a consumer complaint program on the radio. Under attack that afternoon was computer dating. Sandra phoned in her reaction: "Believe me, I have something to tell your audience. Computer dating was for me a gift from God. I am one of the happiest people in the world today because I met my husband through computer dating. As for the price, I paid more for my stereo set than I did for my husband."

Dave Dalworth, a high school math teacher, is 43 years old and recently separated after 21 years of marriage. Dave is perplexed about finding dates. He is reluctant to ask any of the single teachers in his high school for a date. He fears being considered too old by young single girls and he is concerned about his "image". Dave makes a few abortive attempts at attending singles bars. Three nights at these bars yield him only one phone number—that of a young grandmother who didn't care for him. Dave talks to a male confidant about his difficulty in finding dates. His friend suggests computer dating to Dave, noting that people are actually furnished some good leads by this method. Dave's mathematical knowledge leads him to the conclusion that a computer system of meeting people would have to be an improvement over the haphazard system he is now using of frequenting singles bars or waiting for a woman to happen along into his life. Responding to an advertisement in the Sunday paper, Dave enrolls in Date-A-Tronic. He fills out the questionnaire, and mails it in, accompanied by a twenty dollar enrollment fee. Twelve days later, Dave receives the names, addresses, and phone numbers of six females from Date-A-Tronic.

Carole is a wrong number. "Sorry, nobody is presently assigned to that number," explains the recorded message. Dave checks the telephone directory, but Carole is not listed.

Anne is a right number, but a missing person. "Anne doesn't live here anymore," says one of her former roommates. "She moved back with her parents and she told me not to give out her phone number to anybody. Goodbye."

Marian does answer. "Hello, Marian. Uh, I got your name from the computer dating service and I thought I would call you. My name is Dave. I'm a math teacher and the reason I'm calling is that I'm just getting back into the swing of things after being married a long time."

"You say your name is Dave? Well, I'm not accepting anymore calls from that computer dating thing. I had some bad experiences. I have to hang up now."

Laurie is a right number and she does answer after Dave has called four times. Dave repeats the same introductory comments he used with Marian. Laurie, conversation reveals, is a secretary in a large office of an insurance company. Dave and she agree to meet for a drink at 5:15 PM, Tuesday night. "We'll meet right outside the revolving door to the building. I'm short with dark hair, and I wear glasses," says Laurie.

Between 5 and 6:15 P.M., Dave asks ten different girls with dark (or even medium colored) hair if their name is Laurie, but Laurie is not to be found. Laurie is a no-show, but Dave rationalizes that girls you meet in other ways might stand you up also.

Shirley sounds agreeable on the phone. She is warm and responsive to Dave until he mentions the fact that he is separated. "I'm sorry. I never date a married man. If you want, call me when you're divorced." Discouraged and tense, Dave decides to pursue the last number on his list.

Janet sounds promising over the phone. A nurse at a local hospital, she and Dave maintain a fifteen minute dialogue on their first phone call. They agree to meet the next evening for a drink when Janet is through with her shift. Janet is easy to identify; she wears a green dress and stands adjacent to the mail box. Dave and Janet share a pleasant hour over a couple of drinks at a cocktail lounge near the hospital. Dave later escorts Janet back to her car, parked in the hospital parking lot. Both agree that meeting each other was a good experience. Dave invites Janet to a drive-in movie on her next free night. Janet parries Dave's attempt at a kiss, but she nevertheless seems warm and quite interested in seeing him again.

Dave is pleasantly shocked by his experiences at the drive-in movie. Although they have only held hands during the first feature, Janet takes the initiative to unzip Dave's fly during intermission. She requests a handkerchief from Dave and then proceeds to deftly perform fellatio. Awed by the marvels of computer dating, Dave suggests midway through the second feature that they go to his apartment for a drink. Janet hedges and then says, "Sorry, I never go to a man's apartment on a second date. I will go back to your apartment after our next date." Janet again parries Dave's attempt at a kiss goodnight. Confused, Dave makes arrangements to take Janet to dinner the following Sunday evening at seven.

Dave arrives at Janet's apartment. Her roommate answers the door and relays the message that Janet has just begun to get ready. One hour later Janet is ready, offering the apology, "I'm sorry I'm late, but I was delayed."

During dinner, Dave asks for an explanation of why Janet was late. She replies, "My boyfriend and I were out shopping for food this afternoon. We went back to his apartment to drop off the groceries. All of a sudden he got an erection and demanded that we have intercourse. He would have gotten mad if I turned him down, so that's why I'm late. I hope you understand."

Revolted, Dave's first inclination was to run, but he was determined to have sexual intercourse with Janet. Back at his apartment, Janet resisted being undressed. "I'm sorry, I don't know you well enough to have full sexual relations with you." She then proceeded to unzip his fly and repeat her drive-in movie performance.

Dave finally decided to find other ways of meeting women than through Date-A-Tronic. Asked why he did not pursue Janet further, Dave replied, "It was like seeing a sick porno film."

The case histories of Dave Dalworth and Sandra Bernstein are at opposite extremes. Dave is disillusioned about and disappointed with computer dating. Sandra is ecstatically happy. Results from computer dating are quite unpredictable.

The most positive endorsement for computer dating comes from Steve Milgrim, one of the founders of computer dating and president of Operation Match. His records point to 230,000 marriages during one 4½ year period studied.

Negative criticism of computer dating services has been both widespread and vocal. Governmental agencies have investigated many computer dating outfits, and several have been declared fraudulent. Several reasons help explain why so many people have been disappointed with the results of computer dating.

First, very few questionnaires used in computer dating are scientifically designed. It is doubtful that psychologists are consulted to help develop the questions or conduct research about their value. Thus the scientific appearing questionnaire is in reality of unproved value.

Second, few companies make more than the most cursory use of computers. Few dating services really search thousands of files to find you a compatible mate. More often, you are assigned whatever names are available to fit your category. What else can the dating service do? Can they report that because you are so fussy there is nobody in your geographic area that fits your demands?

Third, people joining the computer dating service lie. They distort their age, education, physical attractiveness, and other important facts about themselves. Over ninety percent of people rate themselves as "above average" in attractiveness on dating questionnaires. Lies and distortions are responsible for many embarrassing moments. One five foot nine gal indicated on the questionnaire that she only wanted to meet men six feet or over. Showing up at her door was a pudgy male about five feet seven. Blame could not be assigned to the computer dating service. The short man described himself as "over six feet" on his questionnaire.

Fourth, computer dating on theoretical grounds is a sound idea. If the questions were good and thousands of different types of people joined computer dating, we would have a scientifically sound way of matching people. Unfortunately, not only are the questions sometimes unrevealing, but a narrow sampling of people enroll. More will be said about these people later. With some exceptions, they are not a vibrant, happy group of people. Many people who enroll in computer dating do so for negative reasons. Matchmaking by computer appeals to them because thay have not found good fortune using other methods.

What Kind of Person Joins Computer Dating?

Two personal histories, those of Lola Baxter and Wayne Mead, will give you some insight into the type of person you might meet through computer dating. After that, we will make some generalizations about people who rely upon this type of dating service.

Lola is a thirty-five year old *divorced virgin*. This curious term is chosen for divorced women whose sexual behavior and attitudes are much like those of a young virgin. Lola, a virgin before she met her husband, was unhappily married for ten years. At age 32 she was divorced and had custody of her two children. She works as a medical secretary in a pediatrician's office. Immediately after her divorce she had no interest in meeting men because of her bitter experiences with her husband. Over the past three years her social life has been sparse. One relationship with a 40 year old engineer she met through a relative lasted for two and one half months. During this time, the engineer gave no indication of interest in sex. The relationship ended when George simply never called her again. George's departure prompted Lola to take positive steps to improve her social life.

In launching her campaign to find a man, Lola purchased contact lenses, began a program of physical fitness, had her hair restyled, joined a single's social club, and signed up for International Matchmakers. What Lola failed to do, however, was to question the realism of her attitudes toward adult heterosexual relationships.

International Matchmakers dutifully furnished

Lola with several compatibles. Jim Matthews, a 39 year old middle manager in an insurance company was the first to call. Jim suggested a Saturday night dinner date. As inevitably happens between two FM's (formerly married people), later that evening the conversation turned to attitudes toward sex. Said Lola, "I feel so sorry for young people today. They put so much emphasis on sex that they miss out on the true meaning of love. [Note that Lola has had very little love or sex in her life recently.] I feel quite strongly that sex must come after marriage." Jim was perceptive enough to know that Lola, at a minimum, was saying, "No sex tonight!"

Lola invited Jim into her apartment for a drink on their second date. After necking for awhile, Jim suggested they move to her bedroom. Lola declined, but obligingly removed her dress and bra. She insisted that both she and Jim remain in their underpants. Again, Lola mentioned that sexual intercourse should be reserved for marriage. In disbelief, Jim protested, "You can't be serious Lola. Sex is a way adults who like each other communicate today."

Lola replied, "I am an unmarried woman. I don't do things just because other people think it's right."

"But you'll never get to know a man well enough to marry you if you don't go to bed with him."

"I disagree. No man will marry you if he can get what he wants without marrying you."

In bewilderment, Jim left and never called Lola again.

Wayne Mead, our two-date romantic, is a 29 year old accountant who has never been married. He has dated literally hundreds of females since first dating at age 18. Wayne is well dressed, cultured, and well mannered. His apartment fits the stereotyped expectations of the bachelor pad. Multiple stereo speakers are found in the living room, a bar in one corner is amply supplied, and a mirror is placed on the ceiling over a king-sized bed in his bedroom. A housekeeper is hired to clean his apartment once a week. Wayne joined five different computer dating services in the city. His approach to romancing women requires that he be supplied an almost endless number of leads. Mysteriously, no relationship ever lasts more than two or three dates, although most get beyond the first date. Furthermore, girls who have dated Wayne note that he is "smooth and polite." What is Wayne Mead up to and why do all his relationships abort? Let us take a closer look at how Wayne operates.

Wayne telephones Florie Adams, one of the names on his latest list from the computer dating service. His self-introduction works smoothly; he has tried it perhaps thirty-six times in the past.

After briefly introducing himself, he uses this routine: "I'm quite interested in getting together with you socially. I feel that computer dating is a very mature and sensible way of meeting eligible young women. Let me suggest one or two alternative times for us to get together for a drink."

Over the course of two dates with Florie, Wayne delivers some seemingly effective lines. Taken at face value, they make Wayne appear sincere and sensitive. Many lonely girls feel they have finally met somebody worthwhile through computer dating. Note how cool these lines sound. (Of course, they are inserted at different times during a date.)

"You make me realize that mutual understanding is more important than sensuality."

"Florie, meeting you is an exciting adventure."

"What kind of things do you like to do in the
_____?" (Wayne always asks about the fol-
lowing season.) After his date responds with any
activity, even walking, Wayne says, "Good, I'll
enjoy sharing these with you."

"Your face is an esthetic experience."

"It's sharing an experience with you, not what
we do together that counts."

At the end of a first date, if any rapport has been
evident, Wayne delivers his most cherished line:
"I'm just amazed that two people could get to
know each other so well in such a short period of
time."

Poor Wayne, after this handful of well-turned
lines, has shot his wad. With nothing else of significance to say to a date, he goes back to his list of
compatibles for another name to call.

Lola and Wayne are both people with hang-ups,
albeit different kinds. Lola is too rigid to adapt her
values to her present life circumstances. Few men
are willing to tolerate a 35 year old female who
shuns sex unless they have similar values or are
impotent. Wayne is simply afraid of real relationships with women. His rehearsed lines and his
elaborate bachelor pad provide him a phony cloak
of sophistication. Underneath, he is an insecure
person unable to form constructive relationships
with women.

What are most people like who join computer
dating?

Computer dating users are generally in their
late thirties or forties. Many are widows and widowers over 50. About one fourth are age 29 and
below. Most of the unfavorable incidents with
computer dating have involved older people. For

instance, one woman told me that a computer dating service had only found one prospect for her 59 year old mother and he lived 1000 miles away!

Matrimony is the number one object behind joining computer dating. A study by two psychologists in California showed that 92 percent of people who joined one computer dating service said that they hoped to gain marriage from using the service. Only 5 percent reported "dates." This finding helps explain why people you meet through computer dating so often talk about marriage on the first date. One woman received an actual marriage proposal from an older widowed male on their second date.

People using computer dating services have usually tried many other approaches to finding a mate. Computer dating clients often belong to the same group of eager people who join singles clubs, attend singles resorts, and sign up for dance lessons.

Computer dating is not for jet setters, swingers, or hippies. One striking characteristic of most matchmaking by computer clients is that sexually they are quite conservative. Many are highly moralistic and puritanical. (The strange case of Janet is an exception!) Large numbers have strong negative attitudes about sexual relations outside of marriage. A novelist from Brooklyn claims that most women using these services are "sweet, puritanical girls who are looking for an easy way to meet a real gentleman."

Another curious characteristic of computer dating clients is that many are old-fashioned in appearance. Generally their style of dress—even when they purchase new clothing—is about ten years behind current fashions. Should you join computer dating in 1975, the people you meet will remind you of television movies vintage 1965. Hairdos and haircuts of these people are sometimes amusingly antiquated.

Yet another group of people are beginning to explore the possibilities of computer dating. Younger people in some areas are looking upon matchmaking by computer as a way of openly stating, "Look, somehow I haven't happened upon the ideal romance yet. There must be a decent way for two people looking for the same things in life to meet each other." Remember, computer dating in its present form was originated by two Harvard undergraduates!

Some Practical Advice

Should you use computer dating? I would recommend your enrolling in a computer dating service only if you can give an honest "I agree" response to at least three of the following statements. Otherwise, find some other method of meeting people of the opposite sex.

1. Other methods of meeting people have not yet proved effective for me. I need to take some constructive action right now to get started dating again.

2. Upgrading of my social life is paramount on my mind. I do not care if computer dating is not considered an ideal way to meet people.

3. Computer dating would be worthwhile for me even if the people I meet and I are not compatible. I'm just looking to meet people so I can meet their friends and perhaps get some decent dates *that* way. You have to start somewhere.

4. Face it. I'm no jet setter or swinger myself. I would be quite content to meet a nice, mature divorced or separated person with children who is looking for marriage.

5. I'm unattached and I have some time I could devote to improving my social life even if the approach has only a small chance of paying off. My expectations would be low in joining computer dating, so any fun experience that did come about would be welcomed. I'm not easily disappointed.

Chapter 12

MAIL ORDER DATING

A torrid romance can begin with a note to another person. Unlike commercial methods of meeting people, mail order dating gives you the chance to obtain vital information about a prospect before committing yourself to a face-to-face encounter. The romance-by-mail approach thus reduces time spent with incompatible prospects. Unlike computer dating, you are the person who does the matching.

Prospecting for people by mail resembles the methods used by industry in locating job candidates. When a company wants to locate a new chief engineer they correspond with many prospective candidates before having even one face-to-face meeting. An advertisement is placed in a trade magazine or newspaper inviting applicants to write the company and provide extensive information about themselves. As the letters arrive, a company representative looks for good fits between job requirements and job applicants. Personal phone calls are then made to those people whose qualifications match closely those specified in the ad. Invitations to visit the company are extended only to those people who, based on the phone conversation, seem well suited to company requirements.

Companies use mail order prospecting for some of the same reasons many people try mail order dating. Think of the inefficiency involved if a company representative stalked around a trade convention buying drinks for likely looking prospects? Just because a man has the personal appearance of a capable engineer it does not mean that his credentials are those of a good engineer. Yet many men inefficiently spend time and money prospecting for women by offering them drinks based on their appearance alone.

Pursuing the same logic, many companies are hesitant to prospect for job candidates by asking present employees to refer friends to them. Should the friend referred by the employee be grossly unsuited to the job requirements, the company is faced with a delicate human relations problem. How do you say to a faithful employee, "Thanks for sending around your friend but he (or she) is not the type of person we had in mind." How often have you faced the same problem in response to a blind date arranged by a friend?

Inefficiencies and embarrassments involved in many methods of people hunting have provided the impetus for playing the singles game by mail. You can usually find a mail order dating club or "availability for companionship" notice advertised in literary magazines such as the *Saturday Review* or *New York Review of Books*.

How does mail order dating differ from simply running a classified ad in search of companionship? Similarities between the two exist, but one key difference is that mail order dating resembles membership in a club whose purpose is to bring people together. The prime example of this type of club is Single Booklovers, a nationwide operation based in Swarthmore, Pennsylvania. Founded by a happily remarried couple, the club has been adding new members at the rate of thirty per month. Several dating magazines, such as *Little Black Book*, also operate on the pen pal principle.

The basic idea is quite simple. For a modest fee you are entitled to post a brief announcement about yourself and read the announcements posted by other members. When you find somebody you wish to contact, you notify the club. From that point forward, one of two approaches is taken. Either approach will cost you a token fee to contact your prospective pen pal, date, or mate.

One method is for a club representative to directly forward your letter to the person you wish to contact. Single Booklovers uses a more personalized method. They send you a "Personal Profile Sheet"—already completed by each club member —of the person you wish to learn more about. You then correspond directly with your prospect and hopefully inform the club if you two marry. Such good fortune *does* happen.

Happiness Through the Mails

Bunny and Terry, two unattached people, subscribed to the same mail order dating service. Bunny heard about mail order dating from a friend who had successfully played this version of the singles game. Here is how Bunny described herself:

F—3382 (Pittsburg)

29 year old public health nurse with red hair and green eyes, never been married. Active mentally and physically. Enjoy fiction and nonfiction, swimming, all kinds of dancing, tennis, golf. Prefer male under 35 who can relax and enjoy life. Please exchange photo of self.

Terry, also eager to improve his social life, noticed Bunny's ad. But, first, here is how Terry described himself:

M—1897 (Pittsburg)

Reserved gentleman, age 32, very interested in meeting a normal, uncomplicated, single woman who seeks a stable relationship with a mature male. Earn above average income as an accountant. Enjoy all sensible music. Marriage a possibility under the right circumstances.

Terry, after reading Bunny's description of herself, responded. Aside from sounding like the kind of girl he wanted to meet, she was the only female with a Pittsburg address. Terry wrote a brief and honest letter:

Dear F—3382:

I noticed your description in———————————. Although my business is accounting, I consider myself to be a very good judge of people. The things you said about yourself tell me that you are probably the kind of girl I would like to meet. After dating for a good many years I am tired of all those shallow girls who want nothing from a man aside from being taken to nice places. Because of this I have wanted to meet a girl who is "active mentally and physically" as you describe yourself.

I too like to relax and enjoy life. I could enjoy life much more if I had somebody to share my thoughts and feelings with. Besides, there are many things I would like to do together with the right girl, such as dining, visiting museums, taking long walks along the river, shows, and movies.

There is not too much to tell about myself that I have not already put in my notice (M—1897). I am average in appearance, have a college degree from Duquesne University. I am a quiet person who does not socialize as much as most people. My friends and family consider me to be an honest, sincere, and trustworthy person.

If you would like to meet me, please write and send me your phone number and address. As you requested here is a photograph of myself. I had it taken in a photo passport shop just for this purpose.

I hope to meet you in person. Could you send a picture of yourself too?

Yours truly,
Terry Baxter.

Elated by her response from the type of prospect she was hoping to attract, Bunny carefully composed a reply that she hoped would communicate interest, but not over-eagerness.

Dear Terry:

It was a genuinely pleasant surprise to hear from a man of your caliber. This is the first time I have tried anything like this, so I was somewhat skeptical of the kind of person I might be hearing from. I must say, I am not disappointed with either your letter or your photograph. Curiously, I have always admired the methodical mind of an accountant. You people seem to do things in such a logical way.

You mention that you are a quiet person. Do not be concerned about that. It is my firm opinion that too many people these days are not quiet enough. They shoot off their mouths long before their minds are loaded! You mention that walking by the river is an activity you would like to share with a girl. I too think that walks along the river give one time for quiet reflection; something that people need to do more of today.

I would not at all be opposed to meeting you. Perhaps you could call me some time. I can most easily be reached evenings after six or Sunday morning.

Warmest regards,
Bunny Turner
(424-3835)

Terry called Bunny three hours after receiving her letter. Within one hour after their first meeting, both could sense a mutual respect and caring. After gently kissing her goodnight, Terry commented, "Bunny, this whole evening has been a really good experience for me. You make me feel like somebody more than just another date." Bunny replied, "You *are*."

Early the next morning, Terry called Bunny with a brief message. "Bunny, this is Terry. I just want to say that last night was really nice. Could we possibly get together again tonight?" "That would be so nice," answered Bunny. After a four month exclusive relationship with each other, Bunny and Terry have established some concrete wedding plans. Some of their unattached friends are now trying *their* luck with mail order dating.

Disaster Through the Mails

Jack and Beverly had a torrid relationship going that fizzled out before it went beyond the letter writing stage. Only a blow-by-blow description can explain how this mail order mishap came to pass. To begin, here is Beverly's capsule description of herself:

F—868 (Boston)
Exceedingly attractive, personable, intelligent, and well educated woman of 26. Long, shiny black hair, statuesque figure, blue eyes. Administrative assistant to president of large company. Interests are many and varied including classical literature, reading and

writing poetry, scuba diving, horseback riding, chess, violin. Formerly married, but now single in spirit and philosophy. Searching for sensitive, exceptionally bright, creative, attractive male with strong interest in marriage and 100% fidelity.

Jack also presented a very positive description of himself:

M—917 (Hartford)

Dynamic and aggressive 35 year old attorney, divorced, one child, modern liberated male without any hangups about putting women down. Enthusiastic about water and snow skiing, golf, hiking, guitar playing. Avid reader, currently writing serious novel. Looking for serious-minded, yet fun-loving woman to share new experiences with. Appearance less important than intellect or emotional depth.

Jack felt that the person coded as 868 and he had enough in common to warrant writing a letter. The "100% fidelity" requirement sounded out of keeping with Beverly's general description, but Jack was not deterred from exploring further. One Sunday afternoon he typed a letter to female 868:

September 14

Dear Member 868, whoever you are:

Your brief description contained in the club newsletter sounds exceptional from my point of view. What man of my age and background would not be interested in meeting an "exceedingly attractive, personable woman of 26?" It is obvious from the comments you made about yourself that you take both your social life and career seriously. People like you are rare.

You are probably wondering why a 35 year

old lawyer has to find romance through the mails. What you probably do not realize is that it is very difficult to meet women in Hartford, Connecticut. It is a very unsocial town. There are a few singles bars, but I do not enjoy that kind of scene. Almost all the girls I run into at parties or through friends work for insurance companies. (If you live in Hartford long enough, you prefer to avoid anybody connected with the insurance business. It is so drab.) But even if I lived in a large city, it would still be difficult for me to meet the woman I seek. The type of woman I demand and need is a rare commodity.

My personal situation is in good shape. My former wife has remarried and our little girl has accepted the situation. My career with the law firm is progressing quite well. There is talk that I may be up for a partnership by the first of the year. My income allows me to enjoy a wide variety of entertainment. I have all the *material* pleasures I care about. The missing element is a deep spiritual relationship with the right woman. Marriage is also on my mind, providing I find a relationship that promises an almost nirvana-type existence. (Tell me, member 868, am I asking too much out of life?)

I like to get high without the help of artificial stimulants. Good conversation, affection, love, and even sports can get me high. I can also get high just walking in the beautiful countryside or talking to my daughter.

Another significant fact about me is that I am a part-time novelist. For two years I have been pecking away on a novel with an intricate plot. The couple marries, divorces, each remarries, then both again become divorced. In the last chapter they remarry each other. This novel is based on my personal experience with my wife and my law practice.

Member 868, perhaps by now you know enough about me to decide if you want to proceed further. Hartford and Boston are not very far from each other.

I eagerly await your reply.

Fondly,
Jack Demars

Four days after mailing his letter to member 868, Jack received a lengthy reply typed on heavily perfumed, lavender stationery. Jack became a believer in mail order dating after reading his pleasantly scented letter.

September 16

My dear Jack:

Welcome to our friendly club and thank you for taking the first step in writing. Recognize that I am happy to have a wonderful new friend in Hartford, Connecticut. Just two months ago, as irony would have it, I turned down a job as an administrative aide at the largest museum in Hartford. I suspect that a divine force was communicating a mystical message. If I had known about you then, I might have been more inclined to take that position.

Well, despite the time and space factors that presently separate Jack and Beverly, I want you to realize that I value your friendship in light of your refreshing comments which indicate the unique parallels in our interests, desires, tastes, and lifestyles.

Jack, it seems apparent from my reading of

your letter and announcement about yourself that intelligence, sensitivity, ambition, and dedication are a mighty quartet for one human being to possess. How exciting, a lawyer who is also a novelist.

My new found friend, the enclosed photograph supports the statement that I have black hair, blue eyes, and a statuesque figure. As you might infer from the photograph, my vital statistics are: 5'6" tall, 41-27-38 frame, 128 pounds. Please send me a photograph of yourself in your next letter. Perhaps you could include a photograph of your daughter. How old is she? What are her interests?

Allow me to offer some brief notes about myself in order that you might make a sound judgement about continuing the relationship further. (I hope you will forgive my typing this letter, but I want to be sure that you do not wind up in an optometrist's office because of our correspondence.)

While in college, I concentrated my studies in the areas of English and political science. I received a master's degree in administration from Boston University. Then I dabbled in different courses from several leading Boston schools. Among the fields I studied were theatre arts, classical music, communications, and classical literature.

At age 17 I was offered a career as a violinist with a major orchestra, but I chose to pursue a college career. Violin playing has remained an avocation, a decision I have not regretted. I intensely dislike most popular music. But gypsy violin music, red wine and candlelight make a special combination. Interested?

After receiving my master's degree, I took an administrative job in a Boston hospital. I realized quickly that without an M.D. degree I could never advance very far in the hospital field. I learned of an opening for an assistant to the president of a large company in Boston. I applied and was given the job, I assume because of my ability, not my sex. The company's faith in my abilities, despite my youth, has been justified.

Speaking of youth, Jack, although there is a nine year age difference between us, I honestly believe—after reading the characteristics you are seeking in a potential mate—that if two people find one another interesting, exciting, and desirable, and if they have a great deal in common, age is truly a secondary consideration. Do you agree?

In your next letter, I hope you will care enough to tell me anything and everything you think Beverly will enjoy learning and sharing with you. For example, where you attended school, when you will celebrate your next birthday (Bev was born on New Year's Eve!), more about your law practice, why you are interested in remarrying, the number of additional children you might want someday, the kinds of cuisine you enjoy. If you will also share with me your thoughts on the topics of: husband-wife compatibility, romantic love, and (hopefully) the resultant awareness, spontaneity, compassion, and intimacy that could make life truly worthwhile for two sensitive and dynamic human beings seeking a total commitment to each other.

Your ideas and candid reactions, Jack, will be appreciated and valued by this reader. In return, I promise to share my own thoughts on these and many more topics in my next communique. Please do not hesitate to speak your mind and recognize that I will answer all your questions as honestly and factually as possible. I am in the process of divorcing. As we get to know each other better, I perhaps will discuss the circumstances surrounding my divorce with you.

Jack, could you love a girl who believes in God, who loves all religions, and who spends a considerable portion of her day heartfully attempting to implement her philosophy in terms of the thousands of human beings who rely on her rational ability to help make key corporate decisions? Would you feel comfortable with a lady who continues to hope that mankind may soon come to understand the still unrealized promise that organized religions will leave the realm of theoretical mysticism and ceremonial ritual and activate the decision-making processes of society's leaders and followers?

At this moment, Jack, do you feel pity for Beverly because, in your heart, you believe she is foolhardy to verbalize—let alone believe—that her future mate and children will surely know a time when the spiritual emptiness of our people and the social, political, economic, legal and cultural discrepancies of our rat-race, status-seeking society will only be topics for works of historical fiction and/or classical studies in psychology and sociology?

Jack, I am most heartened to note that although you are the twenty-ninth gentleman to contact me through the club, you are amongst the select few whom I have encountered who seem capable of visualizing and interacting with the "right young lady" on other than the obvious physical level. If we ever do plan a get-together, how pleasant (and novel) it might prove to be if Jack turns out to be a man who is not *merely* turned on by Bev's "luscious hair, rhapsodic smile, female curves, and effervescent personality" (to borrow some intriguing phrases recently uttered by one of our fellow club members whose private sexual revolution turned Beverly off!). Please do not be angry with me for being candid. Hormonal activity is great and I thoroughly enjoy being a warm blooded woman—but these are topics for a future discussion.

What I am really trying to communicate at this point is that I truly hope that because you have taken the initiative in writing to me and have willingly tuned in—you will hopefully be totally turned on by the psycho-socio-emotional qualities of my spirit, soul, and mind. It would be a gross misrepresentation on my part to dub myself a psychedelic swinger. And if and when Beverly talks about sexual freedom—she defines her analogies to encompass the whole spectrum of a husband and wife relationship.

Well, my dear new found friend Jack, please understand that I am looking forward to reading your response to my rambling discourse. Perhaps, after we exchange a few frank communiqués and learn more about one another, we can then proceed to decide about an appropriate time for our first meeting.

Warmly and cordially,
Beverly Evan (M—868)

P.S. Do you have a reel or cassette tape recorder? Exchanging tapes, on occasion, would be even more wonderful than a fleeting telephone conversation!!!!

Jack's reaction to Beverly's letter was a mixture of surprise, disbelief, and guarded optimism. Bev's frequent references to sex (or the avoidance thereof) sounded suspicious, but Jack thought that at least on paper Bev sounded like the kind of woman he sought for a serious relationship. He carried the budding romance one step further:

September 21

Dear Beverly:

Thank you so much for your lengthy reply to my letter. Allow me to use my keen legal mind to make some deductions about you. Among the fine qualities you revealed in your letter were femininity (even the scent of your letter was feminine), superb writing skill, excellent typing skill, and a great understanding of human nature. You are delightful on paper, and I hope equally delightful in person.

The photograph you enclosed was much appreciated. My only anatomical question is how does Bev contain those glamazon type measurements in 128 pounds? Are your bones aluminum? You ask so many fascinating questions that I will have to confine this letter to a response to just some of them, plus a look at my expectations in a male-female relationship.

I have enclosed a resumé of my background that I had prepared for professional purposes. The photograph is of Lisa, my daughter, and me on a recent camping trip. My birthday is July 18, and you can decide whether or not we are astrologically compatible. Your age is fine for me; I date young girls out of preference.

Why am I interested in remarrying? Although this bachelor life has a few fringe benefits, I think my life would be more complete if I were totally involved with one woman. I would consent to a monogamous life if I met a sensitive, caring, sharing woman who rated me *numero uno*. Most healthy, normal young women cannot feel totally committed to a man unless he is willing to be her husband and the father of her children. If I loved a healthy, normal, etc. woman, I would have no hesitation about marriage and child rearing. All I demand (ask?) of a potential wife is that she be a divinely romantic (gypsy music, negligee, responsiveness to each other's feelings and so on) beautiful person who cares about me and my career. A woman of mine also has to give me encouragement when I'm down.

Your friend Jack loves intense sex with women he cares about. As for sex, the wilder the better. A perversion to me is something two lovers haven't yet tried. Once you try it and find it mutually satisfying, it is no longer a perversion. State laws be damned (and I'm a lawyer). Sex to me is a byproduct of a relationship marked by rapport. If two mature, heterosexual adults form a constructive, worthwhile relationship, sexual union is inevitable. I see no value in relationships that do not build emotionally. I cannot conceive of a good relationship that in time does not involve sex. I have never resorted to forcing myself upon a woman.

Obviously, you are both romantic and emotional. So am I. Let's keep this relationship alive.

Affectionately,
Jack

P.S. No, I do not have tape equipment, but I can borrow it. In the interim, I may phone you soon.

Elated by her second letter from Jack, Beverly responded with a warmer letter than her first one. However, she pushed hard for answers to certain key questions.

September 26

My dear friend,

First of all, I've unplugged my typewriter —for friends should exchange handwritten efforts. Thank you for the fine photo.

Jack, please know that when I reached the final paragraph of your message, my eyes filled with tears, for your words were as luminous as a sunny watercolor. Beverly's intellect and intuition are telling her head, as well as her heart, that "Hartford Jack" is a totally beautiful human being. I know in my heart that you are a flesh-and-blood *gentleman* who is blessed with that most unique, charismatic personality which brings out the best in others.

Dear one, I truly need to know your comprehensive reactions to "all" of those questions posed in my first letter. To know intimations of the whole makes me yearn for your perspectives in toto. I can only hope that you will choose to open your heart in a spirit of mutual respect and trust. Jack, if either of us settles for less, our attempt to communicate (from the outset) will merely become one more dating by mail psychological tennis match—a fate devoutly to be avoided in view of Beverly's need and desire to find, fall in love with, and wed a wholesome man whose accomplishments are equalled by his personal characteristics of: emotional and intellectual maturity; self-understanding; self-acceptance; self-respect; self-love; inner beauty; inner joy; inner peace; love of life; truth and beauty; a conviction of his purpose in life; unadulterated kindness and gentility; depth of feeling covering the entire emotional spectrum; personal warmth, gentleness, charm, loquaciousness, compassion; love for humanity and justice; total enjoyment of marital sex and—above all else—the deep desire and unswerving determination to totally share himself with Beverly; to love her and be loved by her emotionally and physically. This significantly real, humanistically-oriented male partner hopefully will desire to merge his life and fate with my own and ultimately father the many, beautiful babies, I pray will bless our union and our lives.

Just one more candid remark, dear Jack. Unlike my peers, at this point in my life, I *can* conceive of and value a good relationship that does not involve (nor require) sex between an unmarried man and woman. If you ask me to explain this statement, I shall *sans* coyness ... But first, Jack, if you still care enough to respond to my last series of inquiries, in addition, I must prayerfully ask that you share your frank impressions of the hippie, drop-out, crotch-oriented, drug-saturated subculture which has burgeoned in my generation. Your personal evaluation and response are most important to Beverly. To say the least, I am greatly troubled by Charles Reich's excellent description of what he terms, "Consciousness III." In fact, Jack, I continue to ponder how one actually should define our contemporary, disaffected and alienated (or is it just lonely?), flair-trousered, music-rocked, poppa-hating, street-peopling, stimulant-seeking "mod" generation.

Dearest Jack, with God as my witness, I promise to try to answer your own forthcoming questions in a straightforward and honest manner. I want you to know that I care.

Please realize that I truly appreciate your kindness in signing your message, "affectionately," and—dear one—in wishing you sweet dreams and a happy life, I shall ask God to bless you and your loved ones in all ways.

Your loving friend,
Beverly

P.S. Jack, for the record, may I please know the color of your eyes and hair? (I dream in technicolor!) Good night, "NUMERO UNO AMIGO."

October 1

Dear Beverly:

Thank you so much for your absolutely one-of-a-kind letter. I was both complimented and astounded. The best I can do to satisfy your curiosity is to list your questions in summary form, accompanied by my gut feel reply. You are obviously adamant about knowing my reaction to your pressing questions.

"Daughter's Interests"—Lisa reads books, swims, helps her mother around the house, raises gerbils, collects rocks, ice skates, and bowls.

"Age difference between us"—No problem for me, as I mentioned before. In fact, I would make the scene with a 20-year-old if I could find one who wanted me and whose company I enjoyed.

"Husband-wife compatibility"—Definitely yes. I wouldn't want it any other way. If two people are not truly compatible, their relationship will abort. Life is a joy when two people love each other. I can even brave the storm of a stunning setback in my career if my romantic life is going well.

"Love a believer in God?"—Sure, I'm not bigoted. If a woman goes to church or worships God in her private way, it's fine with me. I won't interfere. Just don't ask me to roll out of bed with her at 8 A.M. on Sunday to attend church.

"Pre-marital sex?"—Are you serious? Can any mature woman expect to date a heterosexual male and not have an affair with him? If a woman isn't turned on enough by a man to have sex with him, she should stop seeing him. If a woman prefers a dildo to a male, that's her decision, but go date somebody other than yours truly.

"Hippie-drop-out, crotch-oriented, etc." — Sometimes I think young people are having all the fun. As I told you, I don't want drugs for myself, but I think those tight-jeaned, long-haired, braless chicks are sexy even if they live better through chemistry. I have no reason to put down young people. My generation, with their bobby sox, trench coats, white bucks, and no involvement in the world outside, were just as screwed up but in a different way.

I hope these answers give you the information you need to decide if we should continue our relationship any further.

> Affectionately(and
> perplexed),
> Jack

Beverly did indeed receive the information she sought. Her letter in response to Jack's candid answers was brief and equally candid.

October 7

Jack:

Your "listing of responses" has short-circuited our pattern of friendly vibrations.

Life is too precious to be wasted by either of us, Jack, so I wish you BON CHANCE in finding "a chick" who is worthy of you.

Your sizzling reply inspires me to confess that I seek a future husband whose humanity attests to mankind's impetus for remaining balanced, no matter what centrifugal pressures tend to pull one off center; remaining strong, no matter what happenings appear at the periphery and tend to threaten chaos. This one human being will be the nucleus of Bev's world, the source and beneficiary of her total love on all levels.

Spontaneous combustion coupled with game playing may appeal to a good many young ladies, but not to Beverly.

> AVE ATQUE VALE, Best wishes
> and farewell,
> Beverly

Who Joins Mail Order Dating

Despite her flamboyant method of self-expression and her neurotic attitudes toward many things, Beverly is similar in one respect to most joiners of mail order dating services. She has basically conventional values. For instance, it is not unusual for a female Single Booklover member to mention her sexual inhibitions in her "Personal Profile." A 42 year old secretary and free lance writer from New York notes that she "dislikes the over emphasis on sex everywhere." A 25 year old librarian from San Francisco says flatly, "I do not believe in pre-marital sex." In addition to being conventional, most subscribers to mail order dating services are well educated and intelligent. Less literate people shy away from having to expose their poor letter writing skills.

What does the typical, average Mrs. or Miss (rarely *Ms.*) mail order dating service subscriber say about herself in an announcement?

F—2452—Bronx. Late 20's, 5'4", white Jewish, attractive, one child. Wish to meet a kind man, 27—40, 5'9" and over, financially secure who wishes to marry a nice old-fashioned girl. Phone and, if available, provide photo.

What does the typical, average, Mr. mail order dating service subscriber say about himself in an announcement?

M—7143—Brooklyn. I am a cultured, personable gentleman, 48, 5'8", 176 lbs., Jewish, professional, divorced, no dependents. Am considerate, kind, discreet. Women find me sincere, trustworthy, and open hearted. Enjoy good dining, theater, art, classical music, dancing, travel, nature, Siamese cats. Have car and can travel anywhere. Please write if your interests are similar. Seek wholesome, affectionate woman up to age 42, compatible for possible marriage. Religion no barrier.

Mail order romantics with more unconventional

tastes can find some items of interest. Your chances of finding somebody bizarre multiply one hundred fold if you do your prospecting in the underground or off-beat press. Check out a newsstand or adult book store in any city. Here are two atypical ads posted in a national dating service.

F—4817—Vermont. Wanted: partner in creating and sharing the good life on my mortgaged Vermont acreage. Gentle, strong person who loves silence, waterfalls, goats, birds, books, and weekday skiing. I am 34, slender, pretty. Mensa level IQ. Please tell me about your dream farm and I will tell you if it is mine.

M—3267—Los Angeles. Want together hippie-type girl, 19-31, Caucasion or oriental, long hair, open mind, from LA. Groovy cat, advanced education, cool, smooth, athlete, 34, hip, quiet but sharp, knows the scene, active in political and social reform. Do you dig way out but honest love, music, modern art, walks, hip culture? Perhaps you're for me. No bigots. Send photo, I'll answer all.

Some Practical Advice

Above all, mail order dating can be fun. Corresponding with somebody you have not met in person has an element of mystery and intrigue. People you feel are obviously unsuited for you, based upon one or two letters or phone calls, can be gently turned off with a polite "I'm no longer available" note. Even more simply, you can discontinue correspondence.

Mail order dating would seem a much less frustrating (and less expensive) method of prospecting than singles resorts or elaborate matchmaking services. An added advantage over resorts is that mail order services supply new leads every month. However, many of the people you meet through the mails will be members of the same crowd you find at resorts and singles clubs.

Suppose after one year of corresponding with a handful of people, you do not locate an exciting, exhilarating romance that transcends any relationship you have previously experienced with another human being? You do not have to renew your subscription.

Chapter 13

KEEPING THE RELATIONSHIP ALIVE

Finding a partner for sex, love, companionship and fun is only the beginning. The search is endless unless you are able to keep a relationship alive. Feelings of frustration, futility, and self-doubt are inevitable if none of your romances extend beyond a few dates. In every aborted relationship somebody asks him or herself, "What's wrong with me? Why can't I hold on to somebody half decent?"

Presented next are twelve suggestions for extending a relationship beyond that initial two week to one month period. I assume you have already followed the Twelve Commandments mentioned in Chapter 2 for attracting another person, and that you are beginning to look toward the future in your new romance. Note that the same guidelines can also be used to keep a relationship pulsating forever (should you be so inclined).

Listen With Enthusiasm

Everybody needs a listener. A major reason almost any relationship goes bad is that somebody is either not listening or being listened to. Perhaps you are now on the loose because your former lover or spouse wouldn't listen to you. Perhaps that new person you are trying to cultivate is available for the same reason. Listen and find out.

Listening is seductive, as brought to my attention by Shirley: "When a fellow listens very carefully to my thoughts and feelings, I find it very sexy. There is something absolutely erogenous about two people really communicating."

Sexual seduction is only a fringe benefit from listening. Another important payoff is that taking turns listening brings two people closer together. One reason people become emotionally attached to their psychotherapists is because the therapist is one person who *actually listens to them*. And good therapists have an uncanny knack of looking vitally interested in most things the patient says.

A concern most people have in the beginnings of a relationship is: "What do I talk about once I've shot my wad about my past, my family, my job, and my interests?" Many people fear a third date because their script usually runs dry after two dates. Others overcome this problem by retreating to group activities or public places where communication between two people is unnecessary, if not impossible. One junior executive, short on conversational skills, takes his dates to high decible night spots mostly to avoid conversation. Some people mistakenly think that once sexual relations begin in a relationship the need for much conversation will diminish.

Listening with an enthusiastic look on your face to your new found friend is the sensible alternative to avoiding conversation. Good listeners— those who listen attentively and look interested —are considered the best conversationalists. Lines such as these will give you listening material:

"I'd very much like to hear about the vacations you've taken in the last several years."

"What experiences in your life have made you such a good and kind person?"

"I'd like to know all about the cars you've owned since you left high school."

Try Good Surprises

A distressing fact about most relationships between two people is that they drift into a routine. After the first several weeks of the get acquainted period, both partners often think, "What in the world do we do with each other now?" Enlivening your relationship with happy surprises is one proven mehod of keeping a romance going. Your personal knowledge of your lover, combined with your own ingenuity, will point you toward an effective bag of surprises. For openers, here is a list of pleasant surprises that you might try until you can develop your own.

Call him during working hours and say, "Let's take a bath together tonight."

Have a photo portrait taken of the two of you together.

Ask her out for dinner on a *Monday* evening.

Send him a Bon Voyage card when he goes out of town on his next business trip (or National Guard Camp or professional meeting).

Name your yacht, cabin cruiser (or dinghy) after her.

Buy him an athletic supporter (large size) and embroider it with his initials.

Shine all her shoes and boots and sprinkle their insides with talcum powder.

Discover a feature about her and make an appropriate comment such as, "Honey, you have the nicest nostrils I have ever seen."

Present him with an intellectual book (not *The Singles Game*).

Good surprises like these can put your relationship on a new dimension and provide you an ample supply of pleasant secrets to share. Bad surprises, however, can shatter most beginning relationships. Here are three good examples of bad surprises:

Announce to your lover you have recently acquired venereal disease but not to worry because you are under medical treatment.

Tell your new girlfriend, who you met Memorial Day, that you will be going fishing with some old friends over July 4th weekend.

Tell your boyfriend of three weeks that you are a virgin and intend to maintain that status until marriage.

Avoid Early Confrontation

Confrontation is inevitable in any genuine relationship between two lovers. Any solid relationship should be able to survive an occasional fight. However, a relationship between two people is similar to a transplanted sapling; its roots have to take hold before it can survive a storm. Common sense and bitter experiences tell most people to wait until a relationship has jelled before having your first fight.

What happened to Len and Elizabeth is typical of many relationships that encountered premature confrontation. Len, a divorced dentist, believed in firmly disciplining children. His new girlfriend, Elizabeth, was a separated mother of four children with a much more permissive attitude toward child rearing. Len was having a drink with Elizabeth in her living room one evening. By 10:30 all the children were still awake. In turn, they would run downstairs to ask their mother a question or say good night again.

Increasingly annoyed, Len blurted out, "Why the hell can't you keep your kids under control? Here it is almost 11 o'clock and your kids are still running around like a bunch of orphans. I hope you don't run your job like you run your children. I want to relax when I'm out at night."

Elizabeth crossfired, "My oldest child was

right about you. You may have a pleasant smile but underneath you're a miserable person. No wonder your wife left you. Who needs a dentist to tell me how to raise children?"

Len and Elizabeth later exchanged apologies, but the damage had been done. Lacking a solid base of pleasant times together to fall back upon, their relationship crumbled.

Ask for Advice

Asking your boyfriend or girlfriend for advice is one of the kindest compliments you can pay him or her. Your actions say that you feel their judgement is so worthwhile that you trust them with matters of major importance to you. Advice seeking thus draws the two of you closer together. In addition, you are automatically providing that person an opportunity to listen attentively, drawing you even closer.

Suppose I ask my lover for advice on something important and I decide not to follow that advice. Will this do more harm than good to the relationship? Probably not. Asking for advice does not inevitably imply that you will *accept* the advice offered. Perhaps you are really only looking for a sounding board. Even this can strengthen a relationship. Here is how it works:

Dorrie: Jim, I need your advice on something important. Can we talk?

Jim: Of course, what's up?

Dorrie: I've been offered a promotion to senior buyer. It's one step above my present job, and the pay would be slightly better. I would make some more contacts in my field.

Jim: That sounds exciting. Your boss must think highly of you.

Dorrie: There is one catch. I would be traveling

much more and sometimes I would be away for a week at a time. Assume that you wanted to spend some time with me and I was out of town. How would you feel about that?

Jim: Dorrie, I can see a lot of potential in our relationship. But you go ahead and take that promotion if you want it. If our relationship keeps going as well as it has been, a few out-of-town trips won't do any damage. In fact, it will make you seem even more glamorous.

Dorrie (three days later): Jim, thanks so much for your help. I turned down the promotion because I feel that if I wait a little longer I may get that floor supervisor's position, which is what I really want. Your advice about doing what's best for my career really helped me make my decision. Thanks for listening to me.

Jim: I'm glad you're glad. I hope it works out. It's a pleasure to try to help you.

Caution: I said ask for advice, not give unsolicited advice. Few people, particularly when a new romance is involved, enthusiastically accept advice they didn't even realize was forthcoming. When your relationship has developed a more solid foundation you can freewheel advice. In the interim give advice in the form of positive questions. Suppose Alice, in Pete's estimation, looks terrible in dark colors. Unless Alice has a thick hide, she will become defensive about unsolicited advice such as, "Alice, you look lousy in dark colors." Pete is less likely to antagonize her if he asks, "Alice you look beautiful in that pink dress. Why don't you wear pastels more often?"

Mandi will raise the hackles on Hal's back if she advises him, "Hal you should get rid of all those dreadful baggy pants." Better received would be the comment, "Hal, why don't you wear the kind of pants that will show off those sexy muscular legs of yours?"

Be Open Sensibly

Pete, Alice, Mandi, and Hal lead us to the next suggestion for keeping a relationship alive. Be sensible in your openness. Admittedly this is the era of confrontation, openness, encounters, and self-disclosure. Nevertheless, people are still sensitive to criticism and have feelings that can be easily hurt. Openness is more palatable when what you say allows your partner some alternatives. For instance, Jerry had enough sense to tell his new girlfriend Sheila that he felt uncomfortable dancing—her favorite form of entertainment. Sheila then was aware of the alternatives facing her. She could (a) drop Jerry for a man who did enjoy dancing, (b) agree to some other mutually satisfying form of entertainment, (c) forget dancing for the present, but hope Jerry decides to improve his dancing at a later date.

Openness also brings two people closer when constructive—or at least not destructive—feelings are expressed. Allen fell in love with Diana. When he asked her if she loved him, Diana replied honestly, "Allen, I consider you a fine person, but I have not fallen in love with you *yet*." Allen could then decide for himself whether or not to continue expressing love to a woman when the feeling was not yet mutual.

What kind of open criticism erodes away at a relationship? Criticizing something your friend can do nothing about is the most senseless and relationship-dampening type of criticism. Larry began a process of decay in his relationship with Judy by his statement, "Judy, my ten year old niece wears a bigger bra than you do." Judy in turn contributed to the demise of their friendship by her retort, "Larry, with a penis as small as yours, I wouldn't comment about my breasts."

Everybody, even the most wholesome-appearing and acting person, has his or her share of erotic fantasies and peculiar thoughts. Self-consciousness or guilt is not in order. You are under no obligation, even in the most open of relationships, to inform your lover of your every fantasy. When your fantasy can only antagonize or frighten your friend and fulfill no constructive purpose, keep that fantasy to yourself. (Or tell somebody about it with whom you are not emotionally involved.) Here is a sampling of fantasies better kept to yourself than shared with your new lover.

"When we are having intercourse, I sometimes think of my last girlfriend (boyfriend)."

"When you slurp your coffee I feel like pushing your face into your cup."

"When you wear slacks and a shirt you remind me of a transvestite I once saw on a television show."

"When you are sleeping your mouth looks like a big dog's vagina."

"There is something about your smile that reminds me of an uncle who tried to rape me when I was thirteen years old."

Allow Breathing Room

Smothering another person can abort almost any relationship. Almost everybody wants to find that idyllic romance they have dreamed of for years. Yet when they do find somebody to love, they still need room to breath and feel in control of their own lives. Unfortunately, what one person sees as smothering, another person might interpret as careful attention. Asking your new lover directly and indirectly how much time away from you he or she needs might help keep your relationship vital.

Elsa, a divorced chemist, and mother of two children, came to feel smothered by her new boyfriend Hank, an insurance salesman. Divorced for seven years, Elsa had carved out a new and busy life for herself. In addition to her work at the laboratory and her homemaking, Elsa regularly played duplicate bridge. She felt Hank showed promise of becoming both a good husband and stepfather.

Hank's attempts to win Elsa's permanent affection backfired. He made sure that he either saw or talked to Elsa every day. When he called at night and Elsa was not home, he pumped her children for an explanation. Despite her protests that it wasn't necessary, he insisted they meet for coffee after her weekly bridge game. Although Elsa and her children had developed a comfortable pattern of spending Sunday afternoons together, he made numerous suggestions for including himself in those plans.

Finally, one Saturday night after returning home from a late dinner, Elsa delivered her goodbye sermon to Hank. "I'm sorry Hank, I really thought I loved you, but I feel smothered. I feel I have to tell you when I'm going to the bathroom."

Smothering sometimes takes the form of one person attempting to substitute love and affection for other normal life activities. Normal people want love, affection, and attention, but normal people also have a large number of mundane chores that are best carried out alone. Kevin and Charlene illustrate how affection that blocks normal activities can smother an otherwise adequate relationship.

Kevin, a car buff, was excited about his new

love, Charlene, but he was also excited about his expensive sports car. Ritualistically, every Saturday afternoon Kevin would clean and tinker with his Pantera. Charlene felt that Kevin's love for his car transcended his love for her. She began to test this love in subtle and not so subtle ways. One Saturday afternoon she asked Kevin to polish her car instead of his. Kevin good naturedly obliged. The following Saturday, Charlene insisted that they spend the afternoon in bed in lieu of tending to his car.

Kevin replied, "Charlene, how about that tomorrow afternoon. The weather report predicts rain then. Today is a nice day to do my car." Charlene retorted with a comment that represented the beginning of the end of their relationship, "Kevin, go sit in your Pantera and masturbate!"

Maintain Separate Identities

Open Marriage—a favorite book of mine partly because it agrees with some ideas in my book, *Women in Transition*—underscores the importance of a couple maintaining separate identities. Two mature people who have struggled all their lives to develop into individuals should not be expected to surrender that individuality because they have found each other. Marriage may give you both the same last name, but you are still two separate, unique, one-of-a-kind, nobody-else-in-the-world-quite-like-you people.

Should you want to look for "we's" in a relationship, there are plenty of healthy ones that will not squelch your chances of keeping the relationship alive. *We* dance, sing, drink beer, dine, play tennis, sleep, kiss, screw, shop, jog, vacation, play cards, sing and so forth together. But *we* do not have to think alike on every issue, vote the same, attend (or not attend) the same church, order the same thing on the menu, think the same sexual position is best, have the same amount of sexual drive, wear the same style clothing, read the same books, like the same relatives, and have the same intelligence or education.

To the extent that you try to merge the identities of two separate mature adults into one, you have begun a divisive force in your relationship. Relationships that pulsate, vibrate, and regenerate are those that allow each other to preserve his or her individuality. The only exceptions to this I know are those old-fashioned couples who met in high school, never knew (in the biblical sense) another adult of the opposite sex and seem perfectly content to remain, "We Dick and Jane Smith, with two children and a dog named Spot." For everybody else, losing your separate identity takes the spark out of your relationship.

Forget The Past

Virtually every adult of the opposite sex you form a relationship with will have one or more previous romances. Many good relationships have been ruined in their early stages by one partner grilling the other about his or her past social life. If you want to date other adults, assume that they have known other people in the past and that they will volunteer this information when they think the time is *appropriate*. Ease into conversations about your lover's past when the timing seems right.

Vance, the keeper of high moral standards (for other people), is a master at putting women on the defensive about their pasts. Obsessed with the idea of marrying a virgin, thirty-nine year old Vance decides by about the third date in a relationship if he wants to pursue a girl for a wife or simply for another conquest. Pity the poor girls Vance thought fell into his "wife" category. Elaine explains how Vance operates.

"Mind you Vance is a smooth fellow. He's good looking and has a good job. He took me to nice places and seemed to think the world of me. I guess you could say we broke up because of his terrible hang-ups about sex. Before dating Vance, I assumed he was a man of the world who had relationships with many women. He and I got along well but I began to wonder if he was really interested in sex.

"Finally I began to understand what was on his mind. Vance kept on asking me questions about my past relationships with men, trying to convince himself that I was a virgin. He pestered me with pointed questions such as, 'What's the longest you have ever been alone with a man?' 'Have you ever taken a vacation with a man?' I really became exasperated when he told me that he was seriously interested in me but wanted to know if I could furnish medical evidence about my not having had past relationships with men.

"I hope for Vance's sake he has found his version of the Virgin Mary by now, but I wasn't about to put up with that horse shit much longer. Despite the good times we had together, it wasn't worth it. I didn't think my past should be on trial for any man."

Karen, a very sensuous high school history teacher, expected her boyfriends to be good lovers by instinct, not by experience. Her interrogations into where and with whom one of her boyfriends developed such an educated tongue precipitated a heated argument that pushed their budding relationship in a downhill direction. Dane describes what happened: "Karen and I were sharing some wine one evening while sitting in my living room. After about an hour of pleasant conversation I motioned toward the bedroom and suggested we take the wine with us. Karen had a quizzical look on her face. She said there was something she wanted to talk to me about.

"Karen sure did have something she wanted to ask me about. She kept pressing for information about how many women I had treated to oral love before her. How honest can you be? I mentioned that I had a little experience along those lines, but she kept pushing me for more specific details. I finally told her I didn't even remember the faces of all the girls I had eaten. Then she told me I was a vulgar bastard and asked to be taken home. Our relationship went to pieces after that incident."

Repeatedly asking your new friend about what went wrong with his or her past romances is another maneuver designed to stunt the growth of your relationship. In time, most people who were hurt in past relationships will want to confide in you about those experiences. Demanding an explanation too early simply places a person on the defensive.

Besides, the explanation you receive about why they split is almost always one sided. Wait for the opportune moment or ask indirect questions to get at the same information. Here are a few indirect probes to try on your lover:

"You are such a nice person. How did he (or she) ever let you get away?"

"What characteristics do you dislike most in a woman (or man)?"

"What do you think really leads most people to break up?"

Enjoy Your Lover's Uniqueness

"Everybody is different" is a widely accepted truth about human behavior, yet so few lovers use this idea to best advantage. Undoubtedly your new boyfriend or girlfriend has many things in common with people you have known before. Also he or she has many unique attributes and habits. Your chances of keeping a relationship alive and growing increase when you respond to this uniqueness in a sensible way. You don't have to tolerate every idiosyncrasy about your new found love, but neither can you expect that person to fit all your preconceived notions of the ideal lover for you.

Nancy irritated Louis, her new boyfriend, by trying to make him conform to her expectation of the domesticated male. Nancy's father and two brothers got their big kicks in life from perching themselves in front of the TV on weekends. Louis, a more physically and mentally energetic type, wanted to help Nancy with chores around the house or go hiking together on Sundays. One sunny fall afternoon Louis asked Nancy to pack a picnic lunch for a hike. Here is what happened:

Nancy responded, "Louis, why can't you be a normal male? I have a big meal planned and I want to cook this afternoon. I bet every other man is watching the football game this afternoon. I called your folks this morning. Mom said Dad and my brothers will be watching the game."

Angered by Nancy's logic, Louis answered, "Tough, Nancy, I refuse to waste a fall afternoon by watching other people do something. I'm not your daddy. I'm not even your brother. Maybe you should spend the afternoon with your father and brothers. I don't think any other man could live up to them in your eyes."

Stereotypes we develop about how males or females should give or receive help can also prevent an otherwise solid relationship from growing. Craig's stereotypes about female dependency short circuited an otherwise healthy relationship with Sylvia. Craig expected a girl to require his help on major and minor matters. Sylvia, a 41 year old bookkeeper, unfortunately for Craig, did not fit into his dependent female stereotype. As Sylvia analyzed her relationship with Craig:

"I really think Craig wanted me to be a helpless, dependent person. Somehow he thought a woman would need his help on almost everything. When I told him I was contemplating buying a new car, he insisted on coming with me to the showrooms to make sure I didn't get a bad deal. When I told him I was capable of buying a car myself, he implied that I would be sorry. After I did buy the car without his advice, he almost forced me to listen to a lecture on car maintenance.

"Craig invited me to dinner on Friday night. I told him I couldn't go because I planned to paint my kitchen that night. Taken back, he almost tried to scold me for attempting such a complicated task myself. I can recall his words: 'Sylvia, painting a kitchen is much more difficult than it sounds. You shouldn't attempt anything so big yourself. We will go to dinner on Friday, then I will help you with your painting on Saturday.' At that point, I began to realize Craig could not tolerate a woman who could fend for herself in life. I hope for his sake he finds a woman who needs his doting over her."

Ask for Dates

As trivial as this advice sounds, it is important because it signifies that you are not taking your new lover for granted. Even if you two have agreed upon an exclusive relationship, it is romantic to extend specific invitations for get-togethers. Remember, just because you have an exclusive relationship it does not mean that you are compelled to see each other every Saturday night (or any other time of the week you consider a guaranteed evening out). A romance between two people is not a contract specifying how frequently you have to see each other.

Asking for dates helps keep relationships alive because it combats the dreadful "what should we do now?" syndrome. Many couples run out of good ideas for things to do together after the first two months of their relationships. "What are we going to do Saturday night?" says she to he. "I don't know, what do you want to do?" says he to she. "Who knows, I thought I would leave that up to you," says she to he. The "what should we do now?" syndrome has taken hold.

Asking for dates is more fun if you do your homework first. Despite complaints of the natives, almost any town has an array of places to go or things to do on dates. (Besides, *where* you go should be secondary to with *whom* you go. When *where* you go becomes of prime importance, your relationship has already started downhill.) Scan the local newspapers; ask your friends and acquaintances about different things to do on dates; check the classified pages in the telephone directory. Four hours of homework should generate a list of at least fifty different possibilities. *Voila,* you can then ask such relationship titillaters as:

"How about a Greek block party next Sunday afternoon?"

"Would you like to go to an estate sale Saturday afternoon?"

"How about a submarine sandwich dinner followed by a visit to night court this Thursday?"

"How about a trip to the county fair Friday. Let's wear jeans."

"Café Baron, an authentic soul food restaurant, just opened. All the other beautiful people in town are going. How about it for Saturday? I'll make reservations."

Remember Little Things

Only social baboons would forget big things about their lovers such as birthdays, the names of their employers, or whether or not they are only children. Little things are harder to remember, but remembering them infuses new life into a relationship. Bruce tromped on the feelings of the woman he loved by forgetting that she had a day off one Friday. Sheila bruised Ralph's sensitive ego by introducing him as an assistant to the president of his company, when his actual title was vice-president. Larry antagonized Paulete when he forgot to ask her how her job promotion interview went that afternoon.

How can you remember all those little things about your boyfriend or girlfriend when you are so busily involved in your own dynamic, supercharged, exciting world? My question practically answers itself. Devote more time to actually listening to what your lover says about himself or herself and less time to thinking about yourself. Most forgetting takes place because you never really *heard* something in the first place.

After you have listened to these little things about your new lover, use a memory-jogging device. Record in a special notebook (or on your desk calendar if you are not easily embarrassed) such crucial facts as:

Midge's period due Friday, the 13th.

Ben to have vasectomy check-up May 21st.

Ginny goes on jury duty July 8th.

Glenn has wisdom tooth extracted November 28th.

Margot begins modern dance class next Thursday.

Improve Your Sex Technique

Competition is getting stiffer in every field, including sex. The quality of the total relationship between two people is still more important than the quality of sex, but people are expecting improved sex lives. Even the legendary sweet young virgin may have high expectations in the sexual realm based on what she has seen in X-rated movies. Your next lover may have attended a Masters and Johnson sex clinic and have developed some relatively sophisticated expectations about sex between two people.

What should you do to meet the competition? Not everybody can become a sexual acrobat, but everybody can improve his or her performance. First, I assume that your relationship with your lover is fundamentally sound; if it isn't good, sex may be an impossibility. Second, you need some fresh ideas. Attend a few sexually explicit movies and read a few sex manuals together. Join a couples group that talks about sexual problems. Attend a sex clinic together. Above all, practice! Adventuresome sex can be one more method of keeping your relationship alive.

CONCLUSION

Quo vadis, Mr., Miss, or Ms. unattached person? Where has playing the singles game taken you? Ardently, I hope that buried somewhere in these 13 chapters has been a new idea or confirmation of an old idea that has helped you, the unattached person, become attached. Hopefully, every unconnected reader has now gathered some useful ideas that will enable him or her to make an exciting connection. Perhaps some commonplace notion illuminated in my last chapter has reversed the direction of your new relationship from downhill to uphill. Perhaps you are now on the verge of receiving the most potent reward for having read this book. One good connection and you may never again have to play the singles game.

SELECTED BOOKS

Nicole Ariana, *How to Pick Up Men!*, Symphony Press, 1970.

Jean Baer, *The Single Girl Goes to Town*, Macmillan, 1968.

Lee Bergman *The Bachelor*, Avon, 1972.

Helen Gurley Brown, *Sex and the Single Girl*, Bernard Geis and Random House, 1964.

Cynthia Buchanan, *Maiden*, Morrow, 1972.

Jim Deane, *The Mistress Book*, Pinnacle, 1972.

Andrew J. DuBrin, *Women in Transition*, Charles C. Thomas, 1972.

Albert Ellis, *The Intelligent Woman's Guide to Manhunting*, Lyle Stuart, 1963.

John Godwin, *The Mating Trade*, Doubleday, 1973.

Will Harvey, *How to Find and Fascinate a Mistress*, Montgomery Street Press, 1971; Pocket Books, 1972.

Morton H. Hunt, *The World of the Formerly Married*, McGraw-Hill, 1966.

Howard B. Lyman, *Single Again*, McKay, 1971.

Nena O'Neill and George O'Neill, *Open Marriage*, M. Evans, 1972.

Vance Packard, *The Sexual Wilderness*, McKay, 1968.

Isabella Taves, *Women Alone*, Funk and Wagnall, 1968.

Eric Weber, *How to Pick Up Girls!*, Symphony Press, 1970.